Ron Proctor

Forgiveness
Fact or Fiction?

Volume 1 - THE CROSS **1**

Copyright © 2017 Ron Proctor
ISBN: 978-1-940359-52-6
Library of Congress Control Number: 2017951499
Published in the United States of America

All rights reserved as permitted under the U. S. Copyright Act of 1976. No part of this publication may be reproduced, distributed, or transmitted in any form or by any means, or stored in a database or retrieval system, without the expressed written permission of the author and publisher.

Original Printing
Copyright © 2011 Ron Proctor

Unless otherwise identified, all Scripture quotations are taken from The Holy Bible, New International Version®, NIV®. Copyright © 1973, 1978, 1984, 2011 by Biblica, Inc.™ Used by permission of Zondervan. All rights reserved worldwide. www.zondervan.com The "NIV" and "New International Version" are trademarks registered in the United States Patent and Trademark Office by Biblica, Inc.™

Published by

Bedford, Texas
www.BurkhartBooks.com

Dedication

To my daughter Deborah, son Josh, and daughter-in-law Kelly, these three have been a tremendous help to me over the years.

To my wonderful grandchildren Caroline, Grace, Madelyn, Jacob, Anna Kate, Emma, Levi, and Isaiah, They are the delight of my life.

To Della, my best friend and sweetheart of over 40 years, I would not be the man I am today without my family.

Forgiveness comes about because of the Cross of Jesus Christ. We walk in and pass out our forgiveness because of what happened at Calvary.

Acknowledgments

A special thanks to these people for helping me to put my thoughts onto these pages: Pam Keith, Peggy Ark, and Dr. Don Black.

As I finished this writing I began to think about the different individuals that God had used in my life to help me with the issue of forgiveness. I have decided to take this opportunity to say thank you to those ten men.

William E Bell Jr
Bill Bright
Ron Dunn
David Ferguson
Don Meredith
Bob Sweeley
Chuck Swindoll
Bruce Walker
Jim Walter
Terry Ward

Contents

Dedication
Acknowledgments
Introduction   9

Chapter One: The Key that Unlocks the Door to a Successful Life   11

Chapter Two: Is Forgiveness a Possibility?   37

Chapter Three: The Day Jesus and I Became Friends   69

Chapter Four: Totally Innocent of Every Charge   93

Chapter Five: God Now Looks at Me Differently   117

Conclusion   145

Final Thoughts   147

About the Author

Introduction

For years I let the devil rob me of my joy of forgiveness. Several years ago I experienced a major breakthrough in being free of condemnation.

I have taught my students and over and over again they have asked "put this information into print." Therefore, I have listened and here it is. I hope it helps you as much as the heavenly Father has helped me with the issue of forgiveness.

To get the maximum results from this process, read a chapter from this text first. Then work through the corresponding lessons in the three-ring notebook. The text was written after the lessons in the three-ringed notebook when my students asked for more clarification about forgiveness.

CHAPTER ONE

The Key that Unlocks the Door to a Successful Life

A few years ago I accepted an invitation to my 40th High School Class Reunion. I had quite a few reservations about being with people from my past. As I walked around the school, I ran into the biggest reason for my concern, my high school friend, Larry. He was my neighbor growing up and the one person that I did not ever want to see again. The reason was simple. Larry knew the old version of me, the version that filled me with shame. When I was in high school Larry, and I had done things for which I felt remorse.

We began to reminisce, and he kept bringing up experiences that I had spent many years trying to forget. Then something came out of Larry's mouth that shocked me, "I have heard that you have gotten very religious since high school."

I answered with a very sheepish, "Yes."

Larry responded with a loud, "Me too!" Larry came into a relationship with Christ after several failed marriages, and he seemed to really enjoy our time together as we discussed our individual spiritual journeys.

As he left to go to dance with his wife, I was reminded of all of the guilt and shame that I had previously felt during and after high school. As I began to calm down, I thought about how grateful I was for that promise in Romans 8.

Romans 8:1 says:

"Therefore there is now no condemnation for those who are in Christ Jesus."

While He was on the cross, Jesus took on the shame and condemnation for the whole world. The verse says that there is no condemnation for those who have accepted Jesus Christ as Savior. Jesus took my past, present, and future guilt and shame away. Now I can live free from condemnation. I no longer have to believe those lies about myself.

God has forgiven me!

Many believers live with a sense of guilt and regret over past sins. That remorse can overwhelm and force them to live a life of shame and condemnation. There are times when we feel that God could never forgive us for what we have done. We feel we have disappointed God. In our minds, our sins are too much, too bad, and too often for us to ever experience God's forgiveness.

One thing many of us may have in common is that many times we do not grasp this important truth: **"Every child of God is forgiven and will always be forgiven."** God is perfect and can only look upon that which is holy. This attribute of God brings up a question in many minds: "Why would God go to all the trouble of creating people who would only disappoint Him with their sin?" Like many people today, we need to understand that because God desires a relationship with us, He does not let our sin get in the way of intimacy with Him. He provides a means of forgiveness.

But for many people, forgiveness is a foreign word. Understanding forgiveness is like trying to get a penny at the bottom of a glass of muddy water. There is something shiny there but getting through all the filth to find it is not an easy task. Living in forgiveness may not be easy, but there is an answer. **The answer is that we must live by faith.**

The Faith Explanation

Hebrews 11:1 defines faith as follows: "Now faith is being sure of what we hope for and certain of what we do not see." According to *Vine's Expository Dictionary of New Testament Words*, the Greek noun *pistis*, and the corresponding verb *pisteuo*, are words used in the New Testament to tell us about faith. The main elements of faith include:

1. **A firm conviction,** producing a full acknowledgment of God's revelation or truth. (*"For this reason God sends them a powerful delusion so that they will believe the lie"* 2 Thessalonians 2:11, 12.)

2. **A personal surrender** to Him. (*"Yet to all who did receive him, to those who believed in his name, he gave the right to become children of God"* John 1:12.)

3. **A conduct inspired by such a surrender.** (*"For we live by faith, not by sight"* 2 Corinthians 5:7.)

As we step out each day, faith gives us something solid to step out on; faith gives us sure footing.

The author of Hebrews explains faith in a very practical way. We trust what God says and place all of our hope in Him and His promises. Faith is choosing to live as though the Bible is true regardless of our circumstances, regardless of our emotions, or regardless of cultural trends. This is a hard truth to live out. Difficult circumstances come into the lives of all people. Grief over a loved one may cause our emotions to soar. The pain of cancer creates suffering and brings questions and fears. Although believers cannot comprehend the reason for all such circumstances, God certainly has the well-being of His children in mind.

Life is like a jigsaw puzzle. Each day of life is like a piece of that puzzle. Working the puzzle by looking at each individual piece is overwhelming. The pieces are so small that they make no sense individually. Once those small pieces are put together, the picture becomes clear. Putting together a puzzle is a process of faith. Though individually nonsensical, the pieces work together to make a great picture.

Similarly, when a Christian learns to live by faith, he learns to trust that God has an amazing plan in mind for him. Learning to live by faith is a choice. Even though we experience circumstances, emotions, and cultural trends that may trip us up, victory lies in choosing to believe that the Bible is true and then stepping out in faith.

As each one of us assembles his own jigsaw puzzle, it is helpful to look at the picture on the box. In life, the Bible is like the picture on that box. God has a plan and a design for each Christian's life. Faith is keeping the Bible as a focus. Faith helps us understand the precise pattern that God commands us to follow.

Most Christians recognize how faith plays a major role in salvation. Believers are taught they are saved by faith. After that, faith is often put to the side. Yet, faith is essential to living the Christian life. Paul says in speaking to believers in 2 Corinthians 5:7, *"we walk by faith, not by sight."* Hebrews 10:38 says, *"the just shall live by faith."* These passages clearly state that faith is critical to living the Christian life, but why are more Christians not walking in faith? The answer is that many Christians **do not know how**.

Ephesians 2:8 proclaims that a person comes into a relationship with Christ by grace through faith. Because of God's love a person can be rightly related to Christ. By believing in the promises of God, we become His children.

But faith does not end there. By grace, through faith, a Christian can begin to walk with Jesus day-by-day and moment-by-moment. Just as he accepted Jesus Christ as Savior by grace through faith, each Christian needs to learn to live in the same manner as stated in Colossians 2:6:

"So then, just as you received Christ Jesus as Lord, continue to live your lives in him."
We must trust that, as we obediently travel down the road of life, God will get us to the place where we need to be.

The Faith Process

Step one in the Faith Process is in knowing what faith really is. Genuine faith never stops with the mind. Genuine faith affects how the believer lives life. James 2:17b says:

"Faith by itself, if not accompanied by action, is dead."

In other words, faith is never merely an intellectual experience; instead, true faith changes life completely. Living the Christian life is like starting one's own business, going to college, or playing sports. Evaluation and reevaluation are ongoing to see what works and what does not work.

Faith Definition:
FAITH IS CHOOSING TO LIVE AS THOUGH THE BIBLE IS TRUE REGARDLESS OF CIRCUMSTANCES, REGARDLESS OF EMOTIONS OR REGARDLESS OF CULTURAL TRENDS.

What does it mean to live as though the Bible is true? It is a choice. Every active person makes choices every day. Routine choices might be to get up when the alarm goes off or to eat healthy or exercise. Obviously, harder choices come into play such as decisions about jobs and family crises. Living by faith may be difficult at first, yet when it becomes a practice, it gets somewhat easier.

Step One:

Each believer must *choose to live as though the Bible is true* regardless of the circumstances in his life, regardless of his emotions, and regardless of the cultural trends that may be influencing his life. That is the first step in the Faith Process; understanding the true faith definition.

Step Two:

Step two is *asking the faith question*. Step two helps the believer turn to the Bible as the object of faith. If the Bible is on one side of a scale and all believers' circumstances, emotions and cultural trends are on the other, which side normally has the most weight to most Christians? The obvious answer is the circumstances, emotions, and cultural trends. In this process, the believer changes that weight distribution to make the Bible the object of his faith. In order to live this way, the believer should begin asking the Faith Question in every situation in life.

Faith Question:
IF I WERE LIVING AS THOUGH THE BIBLE WERE TRUE, THEN HOW WOULD I BE LIVING?

In Romans 12:2, Paul tells believers:

> *"Do not be conformed to this age, but be transformed by the renewing of your mind..."*

Paul connects the way a person thinks to the way a person lives. Paul exhorts the person to reject living life by the world's standards and to think differently. How can a believer change the way he thinks? The answer is in asking the Faith Question. Continually asking and answering the Faith Question leads the believer to a renewed mind and rejection of conformity to this world and its trends.

Each Year, many new books are placed on the shelves of Christian bookstores. The great majority of these books are devoted to helping the Christian live a Christ-like life. Why with all the help that is available to this generation are Christians still struggling with living a successful Christian life? Many believers begin their Christian walk with great enthusiasm. After only a short while they find themselves struggling to live by faith. This all too familiar scenario does not need to exist. God has given believers His Word for guidance.

Step Three:

Step three is asking for the Holy Spirit's help. The believer must realize that he cannot live by faith in the strength of his own free will. 1 John 5:14-17 says:

> *"Now this is the confidence we have before Him: Whenever we ask anything according to His will, He hears us. And if we know that He hears whatever we ask, we know that we have what we have asked Him for."*

God commands obedience. When a believer asks for help in living out God's Word, he can be confident God hears and wants to help. This third step is asking God for help in living out His Word.

Faith Action:
WE MUST ASK GOD FOR HELP.
GOD, I WANT TO APPLY YOUR WORD TO MY LIFE,
BUT I CANNOT DO IT ALONE.
I NEED THE HELP OF THE HOLY SPIRIT.

In the story when Peter walked on water (Matthew 14:22-33), Peter's faith failed him. When Peter became afraid and looked down, he began to sink. Jesus reached out and took his hand. Peter had started out in faith, but the tumultuous circumstances caused his faith to falter. Did he not believe that Jesus was greater than the storm? He had walked with Jesus and seen his miracles. He did believe, but his circumstances and emotions overcame his faith.

Today Christians often find themselves in similar situations. If the believer takes his eyes off Jesus and puts them on his circumstances, his faith will waver, and he may sink. What was Jesus' response to Peter when he looked away? In Matthew 14:31 Jesus said, *"You of little faith. Why did you doubt?"* Did Jesus leave Peter to drown? No, He reached out His hand to give Peter help. Jesus does the same for believers today. He reaches out his hand to help.

In the middle of the storm, Jesus asked Peter to do something supernatural. Peter's fear and doubt were overwhelming. Despite what Peter was experiencing, Jesus told him to take courage and not to be afraid. Then

Jesus told Peter to come to Him and walk on the water. Christians are asked to live out the impossible every day. The only way this can be done is by faith.

> Can we go back to Larry for a minute? My struggle was with guilt, shame, and condemnation. Larry was a reminder of my past sin! I struggled with my past actions and was filled with guilt and shame. As I stood there reviewing over and over in my head Romans 8:1 *"Therefore, there is now no condemnation for those who are in Christ Jesus"* I found myself going back and forth from a reality box to a Biblical box. Reality said "I was guilty" and "I deserved condemnation" but the Biblical box said I was not.

So, is it possible to experience forgiveness of past sins? We believe you are already forgiven if you know Jesus. The problem is many Christians still struggle with knowing that they are forgiven. The key is choosing to live as though the Bible, along with Romans 8:1, is true, regardless of your circumstances. As a Christian, you may have failed, but regardless of how you feel, your guilt and shame are not to be in charge, and regardless of cultural trends, what others could say about your past performance, **if God says you are forgiven then you are forgiven.** Your job is simply to start acting like you are forgiven because God has said so. The matter is settled for all eternity.

Let's ask a very important question.

> "CAN A CHRISTIAN KNOW THAT HE/SHE ARE NOT CONDEMNED BEFORE GOD?"

The Bible states in Romans 8:1:

> *"Therefore, there is now no condemnation for those who are in Christ Jesus."*

The Faith Definition:
FAITH IS CHOOSING TO LIVE AS THOUGH THE BIBLE IS TRUE REGARDLESS OF CIRCUMSTANCES, REGARDLESS OF EMOTIONS AND REGARDLESS OF CULTURAL TRENDS."

The Faith Question:
"IF I WERE LIVING AS THOUGH THE BIBLE WERE TRUE, HOW WOULD I BE LIVING IF ROMANS 8:1 WERE TRUE?"

The Faith Answer:
I WOULD KNOW FOR CERTAIN THAT I HAVE BEEN FORGIVEN BECAUSE THE BIBLE SAYS SO.

The Faith Prayer:
"DEAR GOD, HELP ME TO WALK IN THE ASSURANCE THAT I HAVE BEEN FORGIVEN AND I AM NOT UNDER CONDEMNATION."

GETTING STARTED

Throughout our mentoring study, we will spend a great deal of time exploring the Bible and consistently referring to it; therefore, it is imperative that we spend some time discussing a very important truth about the Bible: Faith.

Hebrews 11:1 defines faith as:

> *"Being sure of what we hope for and certain of what we do not see."*

Although we may not be able to comprehend the reason for all the circumstances in our lives, we can feel certain that our Lord constantly has our well being in mind.

Memory Verse: Write and memorize **Romans 10:17**.

_____

_____

_____

Faith Definition:
FAITH IS CHOOSING TO LIVE AS THOUGH THE BIBLE IS TRUE REGARDLESS OF CIRCUMSTANCES, REGARDLESS OF EMOTIONS OR REGARDLESS OF CULTURAL TRENDS.

Hebrews 11:6a — *But without faith it is impossible to please God.*

Romans 14:23b — *Everything that does not come from faith is sin.*

2 Corinthians 5:7 — *We live by faith, not by sight.*

> **Core Concept:** But without faith it is impossible to please God. Everything that does not come from faith is sin. We live by faith, not by sight.

Look up the following verses in the NIV translation of the Bible and fill in the blanks.

Psalm 18:30

The Word of the Lord is _____

Psalm 19:7

The law of the LORD is _____

Ron Proctor

Psalm 119:160

All Your words are _____

All Your righteous laws are _____

CONSIDER

Try to imagine that your life is like a jigsaw puzzle, and each day of your life is like a piece of that puzzle. When you sit down to work a puzzle, if you try to figure out what the final picture is going to be by looking at each individual piece, you will never be able to figure it out, even if you look at each and every piece. The pieces are so small that they make no sense individually. Yet, once you put those small pieces together, you will know what the picture is supposed to be. When you work a puzzle, you have faith that the pieces, though individually nonsensical, work together to make a great picture.

Similarly, when the Christian learns to live by faith, he or she learns to trust that, even though each day, each circumstance, and each trial may not make sense individually, God has a great, amazing picture in mind. Learning to live by faith is learning to **choose to believe** that the Bible is true. When you learn to live by faith, you learn to choose what God says in His Word over all else.

As you work to assemble the puzzle, the whole process is much easier if you look at the picture on the box. **In life, the Bible is like the box.** God has a plan and a design for your life. If you keep your eyes on the box, you will have a precise pattern to follow. **Keep your eyes on the Bible!**

A visit to a Christian Bookseller's Convention in any year will divulge acres of newly released material. There are enough books released every year to fill an entire football field, row upon row. The great majority of those books are devoted to help the Christian live a Christ-like life; however, the divorce rate among born-again Christian couples is equal to the divorce rate within the non-Christian population.[1] A 2004 study by the Barna Group acknowledges that 60% of people who call themselves born-again Christians believe that living with someone without being married is a morally acceptable behavior.[2] A 2003 study showed that 42% of born-again Christians believe that it is morally acceptable to have a sexual relationship outside of marriage.[3]

DISCUSS *Why, with all the help that is available to this generation, do you think people still struggle with living a successful Christian life? Write your answer below.*

Many begin their Christian walk with great enthusiasm, yet often find that they are struggling to live by faith after only a short while. This all too familiar scenario does not need to be because God has given us **His Word**, by which we can live a fulfilling life.

List some circumstances in your own life with which you are struggling. For example, perhaps you are having financial difficulties, trouble forgiving others or conflicts with your family members.

_____

_____

_____

Even though most of us recognize the role that faith plays at the moment of conversion we seem to forget that faith is also essential to living the Christian life. Paul tells us in his letter to the Corinthians that *"we live by faith, not by sight."*[4] God also makes this clear in Hebrews: "but My righteous one shall live by faith."[5] These passages clearly state that faith is critical to living the Christian life, but what does it mean to "walk by faith?"

We discover in Ephesians 2:8 that we enter the Christian life by grace through faith. This means that it is because of God's kindness that we become rightly related to Christ through faith. It is in believing in the promises of God that we become His children. Colossians 2:6 says, *"Therefore as you have received Christ Jesus the Lord, so walk in Him."*[6]

Ask yourself: How did you begin your Christian life? How do you now live your Christian life?

We walk with Jesus day-by-day, moment-by-moment by grace through faith. Just as we accept Jesus Christ as our Savior by grace through faith, we need to learn to live our lives in the same manner. This will become clear as you discover the Faith Process in the following pages.

What follows is called the "Faith Process." Romans 10:17 tells us: *"So faith comes from hearing, and hearing by the word of God."*[7] Once we begin to renew our minds with what God says in the Bible, then we can learn to trust Him in every area of our lives with all our hearts, rather than leaning on our own understanding. The Faith Process involves three simple yet profound steps that will radically transform the way you live your life. As you apply this process to different areas of your life, you will find that the promises of God are rich and liberating, that the life of faith is indeed a wonderful journey, and that our God is a faithful Father.

DISCUSS *Robert is married and has four children, but he has never learned the Faith Process. Consequently, he has struggled with his Christian walk, and his relationships are strained. Robert has begun to focus on his family members' weaknesses, and an atmosphere of bitterness and hostility has begun to grow in his home.*

Robert is in desperate need of the Faith Process. Can you relate with him? Does any aspect of his life seem similar to yours?

EXPLORE

The Faith Process Step One: Review the Definition

Faith as defined by the Easton's Bible Dictionary, is the "persuasion of the mind that a certain statement is true."[8] Genuine faith, though never stops with the mind. **If faith is genuine, it always affects HOW the believer lives his or her life.** James writes that *"Faith, if it has no works, is dead."*[9] In other words, faith is never merely an intellectual experience; it always changes one's life. The first step is to internalize what is meant by the word "faith." Living by faith is meaningless unless the believer truly understands what "faith" means. A good way to begin the process of internalizing and understanding the life lived by faith is to memorize the definition of faith.

Write and memorize the definition of faith.

_____

_____

_____

_____

Faith is choosing to live as though the Bible is true regardless of circumstances, regardless of emotions or cultural trends.

What does it mean to live as though the Bible is true?

The choice of faith is to choose to live as though Bible is true **regardless of your circumstances, regardless of your emotions, and regardless of the cultural trends that may be influencing your life.**

The Faith Process Step Two: Ask the "Faith Question"

The next step in the Faith Process will help you to turn to the Bible as the object of your faith and begin living as though it is true, regardless of your circumstances, your emotions, or the cultural trends that surround you. In order to live this way, you should begin asking the Faith Question in every situation in your life:

If I were living as though the Bible were true, then how would I be living according to a particular passage?

In Romans 12:2, Paul tells the believers: *"Do not conform any longer to the pattern of this world, but be transformed by the renewing of your mind ...."* Notice how Paul connects the way a person thinks to the way a person lives. In other words, Paul is exhorting us to reject living life according to the world and its standards. The way you reject living life by the world and its standards is by renewing your mind, or changing the way you think. Continually asking the "faith question" will help you to not only renew your mind, but it will also help you in your effort to reject conformity to this world and its trends. Read Romans 12:2 and answer the following questions.

DISCUSS   Should we let the world conform us to how it *thinks?*

What does that mean?

Should we renew our mind?

What does it mean to renew our mind?

If you were living as though Romans 12:2 was true, how would you be living?

Think back to a time when you experienced a season of great stress. Look up Isaiah 26:3. If you had been living as though Isaiah 26:3 were true, how would you have lived during that time of great stress? Write your answer below.

The Faith Process Step Three: Ask for the Holy Spirit's Help

John's epistle contains one of Scripture's most wonderful promises. He writes, *"This is the confidence we have in approaching God: that if we ask anything according to his will, he hears us. And if we know that he hears us-whatever we ask-we know that we have what we asked of him."*[10] Since God is more concerned with our obedience than we are, we should have the confidence that He will hear us when we ask Him to help us live according to His Word, rather than by our circumstances, emotions or cultural trends. The third step is simply to ask the Holy Spirit of God to help you live as though the Bible were true. Just as Jesus reached out His hand and took hold of Peter when his faith was weak, He is ready and willing to do the same for you.

Let us consider the example of Peter when he walked on the water. Read Matthew 14:22-33, and answer the following questions:

What miracle had Jesus just completed?

Why did Jesus send His disciples ahead of Him?

How did Jesus approach His disciples?

Ron Proctor

How did the disciples respond to Jesus?

What did Jesus tell Peter to do?

This story is a perfect illustration of what happens when we live by our circumstances and our own understanding instead of what God says in the Bible. After feeding five thousand men, Jesus sent His disciples ahead of Him in a boat so He could pray. When He finished praying, He walked to His disciples on the water. As He approached, the disciples saw him and were understandably afraid of what they were seeing.

As Peter started walking on the water, he was a perfect example of living by faith. Jesus had given Peter the command to come to Him, and even though his circumstances seemed unusual and even difficult, he chose to believe Jesus' words were true by walking to Him.

He soon began to look at his circumstances, and he began to listen to his emotions and other pressures. To better understand what made Peter sink, identify the following:

What were the circumstances that Peter experienced?

What were the emotions that Peter experienced?

What were the cultural pressures that Peter experienced?

The text remains silent on how the other disciples (who were Peter's culture) were responding to Peter's actions, but it is clear that they did not follow him. The other disciples, many fishermen, understood the danger and death the sea could bring. In a previous situation, similar to this one, the disciple feared that they might drown because of the strong winds and waves.[11] They may even have been telling him to get back in the boat. This peer pressure could represent Peter's cultural circumstance, which would be counter to what Jesus was saying to him. As long as Peter chose to walk by faith, he could walk on water. The very moment he began to let his circumstances (he saw the water) his emotions (he was afraid) and cultural pressures (the peer pressure of the other disciples) become more significant than what Jesus said to him, **he began to sink**.

Any time we take our eyes off Jesus Christ and put them on our circumstances, our faith will waver, and we will begin to sink.

Notice Jesus' response to Peter. He took Peter's hand and said, "You of little faith, why did you doubt?"[12] According to Jesus, why did Peter begin to sink in the water?

Remember that faith is choosing to live as though the Bible is true regardless of circumstances, emotions or cultural trends. Jesus said that Peter began to sink because he had "little faith." Peter did not begin to sink because the wind was blowing or because of what the disciples might have been saying.

Ron Proctor

Based on the verses in Matthew 14:29-31, fill in the following blanks:

Jesus told Peter to _____

_____

Peter began to let his circumstances consume him, and he began to _____

_____

Consider the following chart that illustrates the difference between the reality of Peter's circumstance and what Jesus said to him.

Peter's Circumstance	What Jesus said in Matthew 14:27-29:
Wind was blowing. Asked to do the impossible. Fear was overwhelming. Discouragement was huge.	Take courage. Do not be afraid. Come to Me, Peter.

Peter's circumstance was that he was asked to do the impossible. Peter's fear and discouragement were overwhelming. Despite what Peter was experiencing, Jesus told him to take courage and not to be afraid. Then Jesus told Peter to come to Him. We are asked to live out the impossible everyday. The only way this can be done is by faith.

In this lesson, as we have discussed the faith definition, we have laid a necessary foundation for the other biblical principles that we will discuss in the coming lessons. Throughout this study, you will discover how your relationship with God impacts your relationship with others. Then, you will be able to apply these principles in your own life as you learn to make the decision to choose faith in every situation and circumstance of your life. Instead of acting on what your emotions, circumstances or cultural influences tell you, you are going to learn to trust God and to act on the truth of His Word.

YOUR LIFE TODAY

The Faith Process and the Certainty of Heaven

Let's look at some examples of how to work out this process in the reality of life. There may have been times in your life when you were fearful of what will happen to you when you die. What should you do when you feel fearful about your own death? First, you should recall the faith definition: **Faith is choosing to live as though the Bible is true regardless of circumstances, regardless of emotions or cultural trends.**

Secondly, you should ask the faith question: **If I were living as though 1 John 5:11-13 were true, how would I be living?**

Lastly, you should ask God to help you live as though this were true and to take hold of you, as He did with Peter, when the circumstances of your life are causing you to sink. For example, you could pray something like this:

"Father, since you have promised me in 1 John 5:11-13 that I can live forever with You in Heaven, I am choosing to live as though that is true. Would You help me make the choice to rest in the assurance of Your Word? Please remind me several times a day that I have a promised place in Heaven because of Your Word."

BEFORE YOU FINISH

The Faith Process starts now. Living by faith is a life-changing process; it is a process of choosing of your own volition to live as though the Bible is true regardless of circumstances, emotions or cultural trends. Faith is vitally dependent upon the Bible; therefore, you should make studying the Bible a priority in your life, if it is not already. Start memorizing verses of Scripture that will help you in the Faith Process. Most importantly, begin the process today by asking God to show you areas in your life where you are not already living as though the Bible were true.

Start the Faith Process now. Do it for the rest of your life.

Review *Faith is choosing to live as though the Bible is true regardless of circumstances, regardless of emotions or cultural trends.*

Ask *If you choose to live as though Romans 10:17 is true, how would you be living? How would these truths affect your life?*

Pray *Take a moment to ask God to make these biblical truths a greater reality in your attitudes and actions. Share your thoughts below.*

Consider all the material through which you have just worked, and read the following statement. When you completely agree with the statement, sign on the line.

> Today, I am making a new commitment to choose to live as though the Bible is true regardless of my circumstances, my emotions and the cultural trends in my life. I know that I can do this by the power of God's Holy Spirit.
>
> Signed: _____

---

[1] The Barna Group www.bama.org
[2] ibid.
[3] ibid.
[4] 2 Corinthians 5:7
[5] Hebrews 10:38
[6] NASB
[7] NKN
[8] Easton, M.G., M.A.D.D., Easton's Bible Dictionary, (Oak Harbor, WA: Logos Research Systems, Inc.) 1996
[9] James 2:17, NASB
[10] 1John 5:14-15
[11] Matthew 8:23-26
[12] Matthew 14:31

NOTES:

CHAPTER TWO

Is Forgiveness a Possibility?

One day I was sitting in my office, and I heard a soft knock on the door. In walked a young college student in tears. I invited her in and asked if there was some way I could help her. She said, "All of my life I have felt guilty. I was saved when I was nine. I understand that Jesus died for my sin. Why do I still feel guilty for my sin? I hear people talking and singing about being free, but I don't know what that is!" As I listened, I realized that Debra had spent all of her life trying to find forgiveness. To her, forgiveness was fictitious. People called her by the name Debra, but that was the one thing, grace, that she couldn't get a handle on. She needed to understand the meaning of redemption that leads to knowing she has been forgiven. This chapter deals with the understanding Debra needed in order to find the truth about forgiveness and how to forgive others.

PROPITIATION

Propitiation is to satisfy or appease a holy God by turning away His wrath. The best one-word definition of propitiation is "satisfaction." In order to forgive others, it is important to understand the vast truth of God's forgiveness.

37

The *Holman Illustrated Bible Dictionary* states as follows: "Propitiation ... speaks of the appeasement of an offended party—specifically the Christian God—from wrath or anger."

The expression, "the wrath of God," is mentioned in the Old Testament over five hundred times. God is offended by man's sin. He is a holy and just God who cannot look on sin. The Old Testament tells of many times when man's sin brought about God's wrath.

In the beginning, when Adam and Eve chose to disobey God, He responded in wrath. He banished them from the beautiful garden He had prepared for them.

> *"To Adam the LORD God said, "Because you listened to your wife and ate from the tree about which I commanded you, 'You must not eat of it,' Cursed is the ground because of you; through painful toil you will eat of it all the days of your life. It will produce thorns and thistles for you, and you will eat the plants of the field. By the sweat of your brow you will eat your food until you return to the ground, since from it you were taken; for dust you are and to dust you will return."*
> Genesis 3:17-19

> *"To the woman the LORD God said, "I will greatly increase your pains in childbearing; with pain you give birth to children. Your desire will be for your husband, and he will rule over you."*
> Genesis 3:16

In the *MacArthur Study Bible*, John MacArthur writes as follows regarding Genesis 3:16:

"... because of sin and the curse, the man and the woman will face struggles in their own relationship. Sin has turned the harmonious system of God-ordained roles into distasteful struggles of self-will. Lifelong companions will need God's help in getting along ..."

In the *Jeremiah Study Bible*, David Jeremiah writes as follows:

"With the curse on humanity came five tragic realities: sorrow, pain, relational discord, sweat, and death."

It was Adam who is held accountable for bringing sin and death into the world. (*"For as in Adam all die, so in Christ all will be made alive"* 1 Corinthians 15:22.) Eve sinned first, but she was deceived. Adam was not deceived. Adam's sin was purposeful. (*"And Adam was not the one deceived; it was the woman who was deceived and became a sinner"* 1 Timothy 2:14.)

By the time of Noah, man's wickedness had increased greatly. "The LORD saw how great man's wickedness on the earth had become, and that every inclination of the thoughts of his heart was only evil all the time. The LORD was grieved that he had made man on the earth, and his heart was filled with pain. So the LORD said:

"I will wipe mankind, whom I have created, from the face of the earth— men and animals, and creatures that move along the ground, and birds of the air— for I am grieved that I have made them."
But Noah found favor in the eyes of the LORD.

> *("The LORD saw how great the wickedness of the human race had become on the earth, and that every inclination of the thoughts of the human heart was only evil all the time.*
> *The LORD regretted that he had made human beings on the earth, and his heart was deeply troubled. So the LORD said, 'I will wipe from the face of the earth the human race I have created—and with them the animals, the birds and the creatures that move along the ground—for I regret that I have made them.' But Noah found favor in the eyes of the LORD."*
>
> Genesis 6:5-8

Noah built an ark as God directed; he and his family were saved from the flood.

Because God is a just and righteous God, He must punish sin. In the Old Testament, after the sin of the Israelites with the golden calf at Mount Sinai, there was a provisional "tent of meeting" constructed, a tabernacle where God met with Moses outside the camp.(*"Now Moses used to take a tent and pitch it outside the camp some distance away, calling it the 'tent of meeting.' Anyone inquiring of the LORD would go to the tent of meeting outside the camp"* Exodus 33:7.) Later on, there was another tabernacle built with donations of material from the people (Exodus 25:1-9) and in accordance with directions given by God (Exodus 26). An altar of burnt offering was constructed (Exodus 27:1-8). Specifications were given for a courtyard around the tabernacle (Exodus 27:9-19) and the priestly garments (Exodus 28). There are many other regulations from God detailed in the books of Exodus and Leviticus.

God's character was satisfied, once a year, on the Day of Atonement (Leviticus chapter 16). On that day, the high priest performed elaborate rituals to atone for the sins of the people. The high priest was told what to wear and what offerings to bring. Besides the other animals, he was to take two goats and cast lots for the goats. The high priest was to bring the goat whose lot fell to the LORD and sacrifice it for a sin offering. The goat chosen by lot as the scapegoat was to be presented alive before the LORD to be used for making atonement by sending it into the desert. Release of the goat into the wild represented the taking away of sin. The high priest and the man who released the scapegoat were told how to remove their clothes and how to bathe. The Jews still observe the day and call it "Yom Kippur," a holy day marked by fasting and prayer for the atonement of sins.

The people were given instructions on how to build the Ark of the Covenant. The mercy seat sat atop the Ark. On the Day of Atonement, the priest was to slaughter a bull for his own sin offering and sprinkle blood on the mercy seat. Then he was to slaughter the goat for the sin offering for the people and sprinkle its blood as he had the bull's blood. The Greek word for propitiation is *hilasterion*. The same word is used for the mercy seat in Hebrew. The mercy seat was the place where God's wrath for sins was satisfied. Also within the Ark of the Covenant were Aaron's Rod, the Tablets on which the finger of God had written the Commandments, and the Manna. Aaron's rod that budded was kept as a sign of authority to the rebellious Israelites; it was to put an end to their grumbling (*"The LORD said to Moses, 'Put back Aaron's staff in front of the ark of the covenant law, to be kept as a sign to the rebellious. This will put an end to their grumbling against me, so that they will not die'"* Numbers 17:10). The Tablets represented God's standard of holiness. The Manna represented the faithfulness of the Lord in caring for His people.

As mentioned before, the Day of Atonement was an annual event. Once a year, on that specified day, forgiveness was granted to the people of Israel. However, the effects of those sacrifices were only temporary. They had to be repeated every year. There were other sacrifices throughout the year. Through His love, mercy, and grace, God established a means by which His people could offer a lamb as the sacrifice of atonement and cover their sins. When the life of an innocent animal was sacrificed to cover the sins of the people, God's justice, righteousness, goodness and all His attributes were satisfied. The relationship between the Father and His people could remain intimate.

The Bible is full of stories exemplifying God's redemptive love. Ruth was a widow. The book of Ruth describes Boaz as her "kinsman redeemer." He was a close relative of her dead husband. When Boaz took Ruth to be his wife, it was God's amazing way of taking care of her needs, both in this life and in the life to come.

The prophet Hosea married a woman named Gomer. Despite Hosea's love and care, Gomer was unfaithful and left him to become a harlot. Hosea felt betrayed and heartbroken, but he never stopped loving Gomer. Years later, Hosea found a filthy Haggard for sale in the slave market. Those feelings of betrayal were still there but Hosea cared for her. Hosea was intentional about his love for Gomer. He purchased her from the slave market. He took her home. After a time of cleansing, he restored her to her place as his wife. Even though she had betrayed him in the worst possible way someone could betray a spouse, he saved her from a life of abuse, neglect, and humiliation.

Now fast forward from the Old Testament to the New Testament. The Old Testament tells about the time before Christ. There is a new story and a new way of life after Jesus came to earth. Jesus lived on this earth thirty-three years and was crucified, making atonement for our sins. Jesus Christ' death satisfied God's justice and righteousness. Through the crucifixion of Jesus, God extended that same opportunity for forgiveness and relationship to anyone who would accept the sacrifice of the innocent Christ for their sins.

The Bible says in John 3:16 that God so loved the world that He sent His only begotten Son so that whoever believes in Him will never perish but have everlasting life. Christ's blood satisfied God's holiness and justice. Only begotten means *same essence*. Christ's crucifixion and resurrection changed everything.

Christ's death lays the foundation for the doctrine of propitiation; it satisfied the offense of God's righteousness and God's justice. God's wrath was turned away for all of eternity because of the death of Jesus Christ. Jesus' crucifixion communicated to the entire world that God's offended character had been appeased. The Cross of Jesus Christ became the permanent **satisfaction** for all of man's sin.

> *"Unlike the other high priests, he does not need to offer sacrifices day after day, first for his own sins, and then for the sins of the people. He sacrificed for their sins once for all when he offered himself."*
> Hebrews 7:27

Faith Definition:
FAITH IS CHOOSING TO LIVE AS THOUGH THE BIBLE IS TRUE REGARDLESS OF CIRCUMSTANCES, REGARDLESS OF EMOTIONS OR REGARDLESS OF CULTURAL TRENDS.

1 John 4:10 says:

> "Herein is love, not that we loved God, but that He loved us, and sent his Son to be the propitiation for our sins."

Applying the faith process starts with believing that 1 John 4:10 is true, no matter what circumstances occur or emotions arise or cultural trends surface. How does that apply to the life of a believer? God's anger was satisfied through Christ's death on the cross. God sees the believer as having never sinned and as perfectly righteous as Christ Himself is righteous. The believer can rest assured that he is righteous before God and God is satisfied with him. God looks at the believer through the lens of satisfaction. Why? Because of Christ's death and resurrection.

In the first century, when a criminal was imprisoned, a certificate of debt was displayed on his cell door. The certificate listed the criminal's offense and his sentence. Once the sentence was fulfilled, the word *"Tetelestai"* was written across the certificate. The person who had once been imprisoned would keep that certificate with him to prove that he had paid his debt.

The word *"Tetelestai"* means **"paid in full."** As Christ hung on the cross dying, He shouted the word *"Tetelestai"* meaning **"it is finished."** No one has to pay the required sentence for his sins. Every believer can walk through his life secure in the knowledge that the certificate of debt has the word *"Tetelestai"* written in the blood of Jesus across the front.

Colossians 2:13-14 says:

> "When you were dead in your sins and in the uncircumcision of your flesh, God made you alive

with Christ. He forgave us all our sins, having canceled the charge of our legal indebtedness, which stood against us and condemned us; he has taken it away, nailing it to the cross."

Living as though that is true, a believer can live a life of freedom because God has canceled his debt and nailed it to the cross.

REDEMPTION

The doctrine of Redemption says that Christians have been set free from the bondage and penalty of sin because they have been purchased with the blood of Jesus Christ.

According to *Vine's Expository Dictionary of New Testament Words*, *Exagorazo* means to buy or buy out, especially with purchasing a slave with a view to his freedom. *Exagorazo* is based on the Greek word agora. In the Roman world of the first century, every major city had an agora or marketplace. In the marketplace, people could buy things including human slaves. When purchased, the slave was redeemed or delivered from the slave market.

Ephesians 1:7 says:

> *"In him we have redemption through His blood, the forgiveness of sins, in accordance with the riches of God's grace."*

FAITH DEFINITION:
FAITH IS CHOOSING TO LIVE AS THOUGH THE BIBLE IS TRUE REGARDLESS OF CIRCUMSTANCES, REGARDLESS OF EMOTIONS OR REGARDLESS OF CULTURAL TRENDS.

According to the Faith Definition above and in accordance to Ephesians 1:7, all true believers are redeemed or set free through the blood of Jesus. That redemption includes total forgiveness of sins. Believers can bask in the riches of God's grace. Since the Bible is true, no matter the circumstances, emotions, or cultural trends, Christians can be assured they are redeemed or set free from the chains of sin. They are free to respond to others with that same forgiveness.

In this world, mankind is ruled by the Deceiver and overwhelmed by a desolate condition. It is not uncommon in a conversation about world events to hear someone ask, "What is going on in this world?" "Why is there so much hatred in this world?" "What is wrong with people today?" The answer to these incredibly complex questions is relatively simple. Man is in slavery to sin.

Sin is anything done or not done that displeases God. As residents on this planet, man is under the rule of Satan. Just as in the slave market described previously, man is in slavery to Satan and cursed by sin. The situation is too grave and too big for man to handle alone. As a fallen being, man is on display, vulnerable and ashamed. Therefore, the only hope is for a Redeemer to come to reclaim us from the clutches of Satan. That is precisely what Jesus Christ did.

Romans 5:8 says:

> *"But God demonstrates his own love for us in this: While we were still sinners, Christ died for us."*

This verse tells how much God's love was poured out when his son died for all of mankind. Man does not have to clean up to come to God. God takes us as we are and begins to change us. In love, God reclaimed man from the slave market of sin. God guarantees that believers will never be resold into the slave market. Through his redeeming love, he shows how valuable his followers are to him. No matter what circumstances, emotions or cultural trends face a believer, God is still faithful to this promise.

If a Christian is set free from bondage, then how does that apply to his relationships with others? Christ has not just redeemed mankind for the sake of his relationship with God. The **Doctrine of Redemption** translates into relationships with others as well. Forgiveness of others is a choice. But the choice is only possible because of what God has done.

FORGIVING OTHERS
UNDERSTANDING PROPITIATION IS THE CONDUIT TO FORGIVING OTHERS. THE KEY TO UNDERSTANDING HOW TO FORGIVE OTHERS IS TO SEE THAT GOD HAS TOTALLY FORGIVEN US.

A Christian's ability to forgive others correlates directly with his understanding of his own forgiveness. We need to think about what it takes to provide us with our own propitiation. When we've been offended and are angry, what does it take to appease us? We better be careful. James 1:19b, 20 reads as follows:

"Everyone should be quick to listen, slow to speak and slow to become angry, for man's anger does not bring about the righteous life that God desires."

Anger is listed as one of the sins of the flesh. I doubt if any of us wants our lack of forgiveness of others to interfere with our relationship with God Almighty. How can I be so filled with pride that appeasement of my own anger takes more effort than God says it should take?

God looks at man through Christ's redemptive work and sees him the same way He sees His Son. Because of God's redemptive work, man is seen as holy, forgiven and without sin. True peace comes when one realizes that he has been forgiven because of the death of Jesus. **Christians forgive because they realize how much they have been forgiven.** Man's willingness to forgive others stems from gratitude to God for the forgiveness he has been given. The throne of judgment became a place of mercy. We need to apply that same mercy to others.

Ephesians 4:32 explains the extension of forgiveness in this way:

> *"Be kind and compassionate to one another,*
> *forgiving each other,*
> *just as in Christ God forgave you."*

If one believes Ephesians 4:32 is true, how would he be living? He would choose to live compassionately and forgiving toward others from whom he has incurred hurt, remembering that he has been forgiven.

The truth is always more important than circumstances, emotions, and cultural trends. Attitudes of harshness, criticism, perfectionism, and legalism arise that make believers harbor resentment and have unhealthy relationships. However, these problems are secondary issues. These attitudes are only surface problems. They can only be addressed by dealing with the core issue, which is a sinful attitude, including an inability to grasp the truth of Christ's forgiveness.

Man simply cannot forgive others until he has embraced his own forgiveness. This is possible by practicing Romans 12:2 which says to renew your mind. When it comes to forgiveness, the renewing of the mind is a matter of practicing the faith process:

Step 1:

Review the definition. Faith is choosing to live as though the Bible is true regardless of circumstances, regardless of emotions or regardless of cultural trends.

Step 2:

Ask the Faith Question. "If I were living as though Romans 12:2 were true, how would I be living?"

Answer: I would be renewing my mind.

Step 3:

Ask for the Holy Spirit's help.

Individual believers sometimes struggle with the reality that we have been forgiven. Believers also struggle with forgiving others. Some members of the body of Christ do not understand forgiveness. **One cannot impart what he does not possess.** Many people in the body of Christ have a 50/50 mentality meaning that *if you do your part, I will do mine*. In many situations, no one does his part. People get mad. Feelings are hurt. With the 50/50 mentality, forgiveness may not occur. Christians have a decision to make. We need to choose to forgive because God has forgiven us. We need to do the right thing because He commands us to do so. For example, in the Bible we are each told how to treat our spouse. I don't see anything there that says it is okay for me to become angry with my wife if my wife is angry with me.

People in the body of Christ may expect others to be perfect. What happens? One person lets the other down. That person gets angry. They part ways, sometimes even moving on to another church. Many times anger is just covered up. Forgiveness may not be a part of dealing with the issue. The bottom line is our churches are filled with believers who have received total forgiveness from God, yet do not understand that forgiveness. Therefore, the body of Christ is not passing that forgiveness along to others.

Sometimes Christians involve themselves in activity after activity trying to win the favor of God. This happens in churches. Believers try to do everything perfectly such as tithing, attending church, and serving others. In doing these things, they think that surely God will be pleased! God does not look at those good works to determine if He loves the believer. If He did, what we do as we live would be disastrous for us. He looks at us through the lens of the cross. Believers can enjoy the truth that the Creator can see what the believer does and still see him as though he is innocent and holy. Our relationship with God is secure, but sin can affect the closeness of the fellowship we have with Him. The desire to obey Him should come from gratitude for what God has done for us.

Even though believers still sin, and we are repentant and are forgiven, God might let us suffer the earthly consequences of our sin. God will always look at us through a lens of satisfaction because of the blood of Jesus Christ. God loves us in spite of our sins.

FAITH, FACT, FEELING

Faith feeds the facts. Feelings follow.

If these words were cars in a train, **FACT** would be the engine, **FAITH** the fuel car, and **FEELINGS** the caboose. As the Christian responds to circumstances, emotions, and cultural trends, sometimes these train cars get off track and out of order. The caboose or feelings try to run ahead of the engine, truth. The truth in God's Word should always overcome the passion aroused by a believer's feelings. God's truth fuels the Christian's faith, which overrules anything else.

The truth lies here: Once the believer understands the truth of propitiation, he is freed to serve God with pure motives. The Christian is also freed to forgive anyone who needs his forgiveness. All decisions are based on the truth of God's Word instead of facts or feelings.

Through much time of understanding, the young lady, Debra, began to unload her guilt and see all Christ had done for her and how God looks at her through the shed blood of Jesus Christ. She began to see and accept the truth of God's unfailing love and redemption. She accepted that she was no longer a slave to sin but redeemed from that market and set free. As she sang with her friends in church, she could truly sing about her freedom from the chains of sin. She learned to base the way she feels and acts on God's truth and not the other way around.

GETTING STARTED

All of us, without exception, live with guilt and regret over our sins that can overwhelm us and force us to live a life of shame and condemnation. Maybe you have a hard time imagining that God could ever forgive you after all you have done to disappoint him. You may have even felt that you have sinned too much, too often and too bad ever to deserve God's forgiveness. Maybe you doubt that you will ever find peace with God.

One thing these doubts have in common is that they do not consider one very important truth: Every Child of God is forgiven and will always be forgiven.

God is perfect and can only look upon that which is holy. It may seem odd then, that He created people He knew would fall short of His standard of holiness at the time He created them. You may ask: Why would He go to all the trouble of creating people who would only disappoint Him with their sin?

Because He desires a relationship with us, He refuses to let our sins get in the way of intimacy with Him. He is so adamant that we be able to experience the depth of His love for us, which He established a means by which we can have an intimate, trusting relationship with Him.

With the enactment of the Old Testament sacrificial system, through His love, mercy, and grace, God established a means by which His people could offer a lamb as the sacrifice of atonement and cover their sins. When the life of an innocent animal was sacrificed to cover the sins of the people, God's justice, righteousness, goodness and all of His attributes were satisfied. The relationship between the Father and His people could remain intimate.

Then, with the sacrifice of Jesus, God extended that same opportunity for atonement and relationship to anyone who would accept the sacrifice of the innocent Christ for their sins.

Christ's death lays the foundation for the doctrine of propitiation (*pro-pish-ee-ay-shun*). The best one-word definition of propitiation is "satisfaction." This means that the death of Jesus Christ satisfies all of God's requirements. God, therefore, looks at us through a lens of satisfaction, and we are free to enjoy a loving relationship with Him for all eternity. His desire is to have a relationship with you, and how you perform can never get in the way of that desire.

Note some key Scriptures:

- *... Whom (Christ) God has set forth to be a propitiation through faith in His blood (Romans 3:25).*

- *... And if any man sins, we have an advocate with the Father, Jesus Christ the righteous (one): And he is the propitiation for our sins, and not for ours only, but also for the sins of the whole world (1 John 2:lb-2).*

- *Herein is love, not that we loved God, but that He loved us, and sent his Son to be the propitiation for our sins (1 John 4:10).*

- *Both the one who makes men holy and those who are made holy are of the same family. So Jesus is not ashamed to call them brothers (Hebrews 2:11).*

Ron Proctor

Memory Verse: Write and memorize 1 John 2:2

_____

_____

_____

_____

Core Concept: God's anger toward us was satisfied through Christ's death on the cross. Now, God sees us as having never sinned and as perfectly righteous as Christ himself is righteous.

CONSIDER

As you read the following story, consider how it relates to the issue of propitiation:

> When Jeremy was a teenager, he was a thief. Most of the time he stole money from friends and family, which he blew on clothes, shoes, music and electronics. However, one time he swiped a diamond ring from his mother's jewelry box that belonged to his grandfather and sold it. When he became a Christian at the age of twenty-five, he repented of his dishonest lifestyle and paid back the money he could, but he could not replace the ring.
>
> Ashamed over what he had done and heartbroken over the fact that he would never be able to replace his grandfather's

ring, Jeremy went to his mother and asked her to forgive him. After he confessed and asked for her forgiveness, she got up and retrieved a small box from her closet, which she handed to him.

When Jeremy opened the box, he saw the ring he had taken from his mother and was sure was lost for good.

"It's for you, Jeremy," his mother told him. "Your granddad always wanted you to have it. I didn't even know it was missing until the owner of the pawnshop showed up here to give it back to me. I've been praying that one day I would be able to give it to you. Now it's yours."

Jeremy took the box and inside with the ring was a bill of sale that had "Paid in Full" stamped across it. He was stunned. Was it possible, he asked himself, that someone would cover his sin and not want anything in return?

Just as someone else had satisfied Jeremy's sin, the death of Jesus Christ satisfies our debt of sin to God.

DISCUSS

How does it make you feel to know that when Jesus died on the cross, he satisfied your debt?

How does that truth motivate you to follow Jesus Christ?

EXPLORE

Look up the following scriptures in the NIV translation and fill in the blanks.

Romans 3:25a: *"God presented Him as a _____ of _____ through _____ in His blood."*

1 John 2:1b-2: *" ... But if anybody does sin, we have one who _____ to the Father in our defense-Jesus Christ, the Righteous One. He is the atoning _____ for our sins, and not only for ours but for the sins of the whole world."*

1 John 4:10: *"This is love: not that we loved God, but that He _____ us and sent his Son as an atoning _____ for our sins.*

Romans 5:1: *"Therefore, since we have been justified _____, we have peace with God through our Lord Jesus Christ."*

What has God declared about us in **Romans 5:1**?

If you were living as though Romans 3:25a, 1 John 2:1b-2, 1 John 4:10 and Romans 5:1 were true, how would you be living?

You might have answered you would be overwhelmed with gratitude. Write a short thank you note to Jesus Christ for what he did for you on the cross.

YOUR LIFE TODAY

Sometimes Christians involve themselves in activity after activity trying to win the favor of God. How many times have you felt the compulsion to do everything perfectly so that you could be worthy of God's love? God does not look at our church attendance, our tithing record or our service (although all might be worthy endeavors) to determine if He will love us; He looks at us through the lens of the cross because of the blood of Jesus. We can enjoy the truth that our Creator can look at us, knowing all that we have done, and still see us as though we are innocent and holy, all because of the blood of Jesus Christ. Therefore our desire to obey Him should come from our gratitude for what He has done for us.

Even though we still sin, and He might let us suffer the earthly consequences of our sin, He will always look at us through a lens of satisfaction because of the blood of Jesus Christ. **God's love for you has nothing to do with your behavior!**

Take a moment to contemplate God's love for you and list five adjectives that describe your feelings about the previous two paragraphs on the lines on the next page.

1. _____
2. _____
3. _____
4. _____
5. _____

Consider the following story: Jill grew up with a father that was verbally and emotionally abusive. She was constantly afraid to do anything that would upset him or make him angry with her for fear that he would fly into a rage and scream at her. When her father called her names such as "stupid" and "loser" she felt small and insignificant —nothing she could do was right and everything she tried failed.

When Jill became a Christian, she had a hard time believing what the Bible says about God being her Heavenly Father who loved her and wanted the best for her. She thought that surely God was disappointed with her over all the mistakes she had made. Thinking this, Jill tried to live as a perfect Christian, doing good things for God and doing her best to follow Him wholeheartedly. However, she still continued to sin, which made her feel shame, guilt and failure even after she confessed her sin to the Lord. Jill believed that her Heavenly Father responded to her like her earthly father based entirely upon her performance.

DISCUSS

How would Jill's relationship with and service to God change if she understood propitiation?

How would she feel about herself? Why?

Walk through the following illustration:

Our sin separates us from God; when He looks at us, He sees our lies, gossip, addictions, greed, selfishness and everything we do that displeases Him.

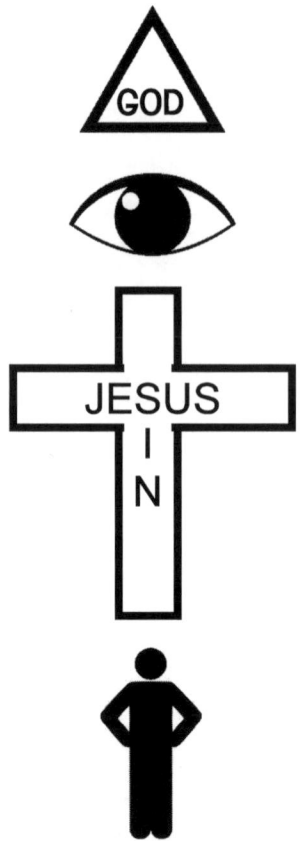

When Jesus died on the cross for our sins, He became the permanent sacrifice. Just as God saw the blood of the animal sacrifice, He now sees the blood of His Son that is covering our transgressions. The blood satisfies His justice, His holiness and His righteousness and all of His characteristics. To get a good visual picture of what propitiation looks like, look at how the picture changes once a person accepts Jesus Christ as his or her savior and His sacrifice becomes the permanent payment for sin. He now looks at us through the lens of the cross. He doesn't see our sin, he sees Jesus.

In the first century, when a criminal was imprisoned, a certificate of debt was displayed on his cell door. The certificate listed the criminal's offense and his sentence. Once the sentence was fulfilled, the word, "Tetelestai" was written across the certificate, and the person who had once been imprisoned would keep that certificate with him to prove that he had paid his debt.*

---

*Be sure to keep this discussion of "Tetelestai" in mind throughout this study; it will be referenced frequently.

In the first century, when a criminal was imprisoned, a certificate of debt was displayed on his cell door. The certificate listed the criminal's offense and his sentence. Once the sentence was fulfilled, the word, "Tetelestai" was written across the certificate, and the person who had once been imprisoned would keep that certificate with him to prove that he had paid his debt. (*Be sure to keep this discussion of "Tetelestai" in mind throughout this study; it will be referenced frequently.*)

The word "Tetelestai" may seem familiar to you, it means, "paid in full." As Christ hung on the cross dying, He shouted the word, "Tetelestai", "It is finished." Now none of us have to pay the required sentence for our sins, and we can walk through our daily lives secure in the knowledge that our own certificates of debt have the word, "Tetelestai" written in the blood of Jesus across the front.

While it is important to intellectually understand the Doctrine of Propitiation, we must choose by faith to believe that God looks at us through the lens of the cross. He has paid the debt in full. When you live as though your own offenses have been forgiven, how will your life be different?

Read 2 Corinthians 5:21.

If you were living as though 2 Corinthians 5:21, how would you be living?

If you were living as though 2 Corinthians 5:21 was true, you would desire a relationship with God because He cares enough about you to send Christ as a sacrifice to give you His righteousness.

Ron Proctor

Consider 2 Corinthians 5:21, and fill in the chart below. Note your perception of your experience in the left box, and the truth of God's Word in the right box:

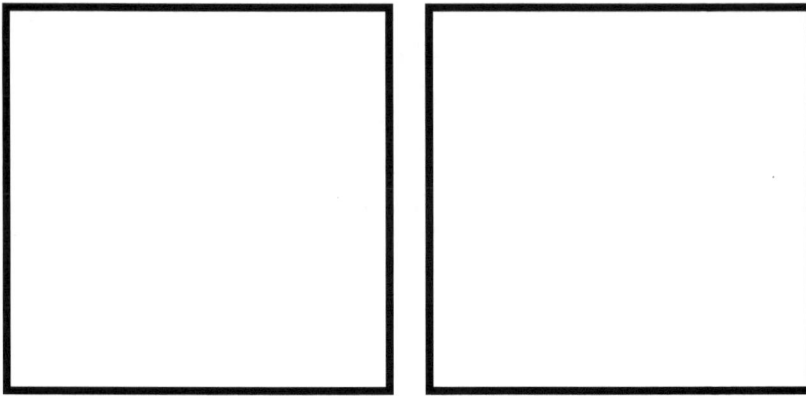

What my experience says about my sin

What God's Word says about my forgiveness in 2 Corinthians 5:21

Read Colossians 2:13-14.

If you were living as though Colossians 2: 13-14 were true, how would you be living?

You might have answered that you would be able to live a life of freedom because God has canceled your debt and nailed to the cross of Jesus.

If you were living as though Ephesians 4:32 were true, how would you be living?

You might have answered that you would be compassionate and forgiving toward others who have hurt you by remembering that you, yourself, have been forgiven.

YOUR LIFE TODAY

Since God looks at you through a lens of righteousness, He now sees you as:

holy

without sin

forgiven

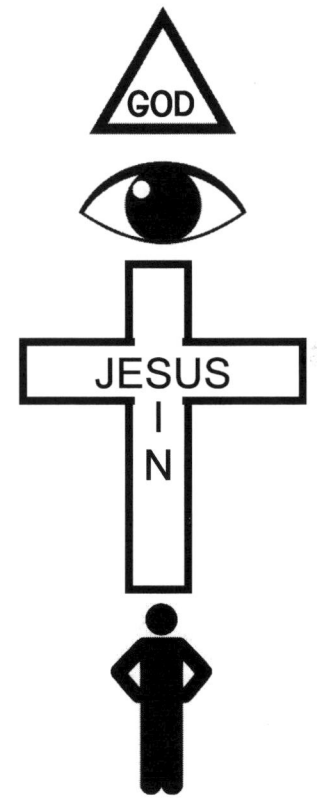

God also looks at other Christians through the same lens of righteousness:

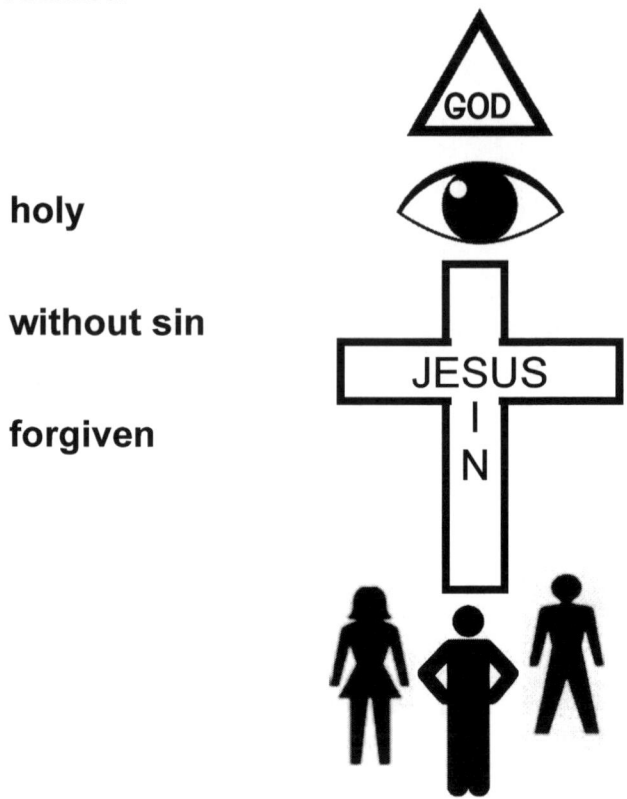

holy

without sin

forgiven

Once the truth of propitiation gets into your personal life, it frees you to serve God with pure motives that are free of the need to earn His approval. Then you are free to forgive anyone who needs your forgiveness.

BEFORE YOU FINISH

God is completely satisfied with you because of the sacrifice of His perfect Lamb. This means that even on your worst days, God is satisfied with you. That satisfaction has nothing to do with you and everything to do with Christ and His death on the cross. The same is true for everyone else. Now, by faith, you have to act upon that truth and live it out each day of your life.

That is not just truth; that is freedom! Does this make you feel grateful?

When you think about propitiation, how do you respond? How will it affect your other relationships? How would this affect the relationships between a husband and wife? Parents and children? The church body?

Consider the material through which you have just worked, and read the following statement. When you completely agree with the statement, sign on the line.

> I choose to believe by faith that I am certain that God looks at me through a lens of righteousness and is satisfied because of the sacrifice of Jesus Christ on the cross.
>
> Signed: _____

NOTES:

CHAPTER THREE

The Day Jesus and I Became Friends

Recently a student came and asked me to visit his grandfather who lives in a nursing home. One day we went to the nursing home to visit him, and we noticed him sitting alone. We went over to talk to him, but he never looked up. We sat down with him, and we began to talk to him. We tried to make small talk for a minute or so before we noticed that we were not even beginning to break down the hard wall he had erected between himself and others. Then we asked him a question. "Would you like to talk about what is bothering you?" At first, he just shrugged it off, and he said, "I am an old man with no hope in my future. I've lived all my life doing one bad thing after another, and now I'm facing the end. How would you feel if you were in my shoes?" He opened the door wide for us to tell him the hope that we have in redeeming hope and that he did not have to live now or in eternity separated from God.

The Doctrine of Original Sin:

NOT ONLY WERE ADAM AND EVE ALIENATED FROM GOD BY THEIR OWN SELFISH CHOICE, BUT SCRIPTURE ALSO TEACHES THAT ADAM'S SIN WAS CHARGED TO OUR ACCOUNT.

"Therefore, just as sin entered the world through one man, and death came through sin, and in this way death came to all men, because all sinned—for before the law was given, sin was in the world. But sin is not taken into account when there is no law. Nevertheless, death reigned from the time of Adam to the time of Moses, even over those who did not sin by breaking a command, as did Adam, who was a pattern of the one to come. But the gift is not like the trespass. For if the many died by the trespass of one man, how much more did God's grace and the gift that came by the grace of one man, Jesus Christ, overflow to the many! Again, the gift of God is not like the result of one man's sin: The judgment followed one sin and brought condemnation, but the gift followed many trespasses and brought justification. For if, by the trespass of one man, death reigned through that one man, how much more will those who receive God's abundant provision of grace and of the gift of righteousness reign in life through one man, Jesus Christ. Consequently, just as the result of one trespass was condemnation for all men, so also the result of one act of righteousness was justification that brings life for all men. For just as through the disobedience of one man the many were made sinners, so also through the obedience of the one man the many will be made righteous."
Romans 5:12-19

"For since death came through a man, the resurrection of the dead comes also through a man. For as in Adam all die, so in Christ all will be made alive."
1 Corinthians 15:21, 22

When Adam sinned, in effect, he declared his independence from his Creator. Reacting to the lies of Satan, who was in the form of a serpent, he and Eve decided that God was indeed trying to oppress them and prevent them from a full and satisfying life. Furthermore, they believed that God was only bluffing when He said that severe consequences would result from disobedience. Adam and Eve decided to go it alone. They would seek happiness and fulfillment apart from God. They did not understand that God wanted to be their friend.

Every person is born in sin. Man does not become a sinner when he sins. He sins because he is inherently a sinner. Sin started with one man making a choice. He chose to disobey the one thing God told him not to do. Choosing to do what God says is wrong or not to do what God says is right, is sin. Sin may appear enticing, but in the end, it bites like a snake. Some people think God wants to keep certain things away from them because He wants to oppress them. What God truly wants is to keep away from us is those things that have disastrous consequences. Sin leads to destruction.

Some people understand sin to be those gross acts of selfishness such as murder, rape, and theft. Some would even say that they do not sin. Consider what the Bible teaches in Romans 3:23:

> "... for all have sinned and fall short of the glory of God."

Consider James 4:17:

> "Anyone, then, who knows the good he ought to do and does not do it, sins."

Anyone who reads and meditates on Scripture, and then looks honestly at himself, will understand the truth of sin.

But isn't it wonderful to know that Scripture teaches the death of Christ redeems man from the slave market of sin and declares man innocent? Romans 6:23 says that the punishment for sin is death, but God has given the gift of eternal life through Jesus Christ our Lord. His death satisfies God's righteous attributes through Christ's penal, substitutionary atonement. His death brings man into fellowship with God.

Romans 5:10 teaches:

> *"For if, when we were God's enemies, we were reconciled to him through the death of his Son, how much more having been reconciled, shall we be saved through his life!"*

God transforms our lives because He loves us. When a man comes to Christ, he makes a choice. That choice is to follow Christ who separates him from sin and places him on God's side. Choosing to follow Christ is an act of obedience.

Dear friends, if our hearts do not condemn us, we have confidence before God and receive from him anything we ask, because we obey his commands and do what pleases him. And this is His command: to believe in the name of His Son, Jesus Christ, and to love one another as He commanded us. Those who obey His commands live in Him and He in them. And this is how we know that He lives in us: We know it by the Spirit He gave us. (I John 3:21-24) Then man can either accept Christ or reject Him and make the choice to continue in sin. That refusal to follow Christ keeps him separate from God. In choosing Christ, man becomes God's friend.

Different Aspects of the Atonement
1. Sacrifice

> *"But now a righteousness from God,
> apart from the law, has been made known,
> to which the Law and the Prophets testify.
> This righteousness from God comes through faith
> in Jesus Christ to all who believe.
> There is no difference, for all have sinned
> and fall short of the glory of God, and are justified
> freely by his grace through the redemption
> that came by Christ Jesus. God presented him as
> a sacrifice of atonement, through faith in
> his blood. He did this to demonstrate his justice,
> because in his forbearance he had left the sins
> committed beforehand unpunished—he did this to
> demonstrate his justice at present,
> so as to be just and the one who justifies those
> who have faith in Jesus."*
> Romans 3:21-26

The Greek word for *"sacrifice"* in this passage is **hilasteerion.** Bauer, Arndt, and Gingrich say the word means that which *expiates or propitiates or a means of expiation, gift to procure expiation. To expiate is "to put an end to," "extinguish the guilt incurred by," or "make amends for."* Vine writes, *"Through His voluntary expiatory sacrifice in the shedding of His blood, under Divine judgment upon sin, and through His Resurrection, Christ has become the Mercy-Seat for His people."*

> *"Unlike the other high priests, he* [Jesus] *does not need to offer sacrifices day after day, first*

> *for his own sins, and then for the sins of the people. He sacrificed for their sins once for all when he offered himself."*
>
> Hebrews 7:27

> *"But now he* [Christ] *has appeared once for all at the end of the ages to do away with sin by the sacrifice of himself."*
>
> Hebrews 9:26b

2. Propitiation

The Holman Illustrated Bible Dictionary states as follows:

> ***"Propitiation*** *... speaks of the appeasement of an offended party—specifically the Christian God—from wrath or anger."*

For more information about propitiation, please see above in chapter two.

3. Reconciliation

The Holman Illustrated Bible Dictionary defines reconciliation as follows:

> *"Bringing together of two parties that are estranged or in dispute. Jesus Christ is the one who brings together God and man, with salvation as the result of the union. Reconciliation basically means 'change' or 'exchange.' The idea is of a change in relationship, an exchange of antagonism for*

goodwill, enmity for friendship. Attitudes are transformed and hostility ceases."

> "Therefore if anyone is in Christ,
> he is a new creation; the old has gone,
> the new has come! All this is from God, who
> reconciled us to himself through Christ and gave
> us the ministry of reconciliation: that God was
> reconciling the world to himself in Christ,
> not counting men's sins against them."
> 2 Corinthians 5:17-19a

Reconciliation is to move man from alienation from God to becoming God's friend; now the believer can fellowship with God. Before believing in Jesus Christ as Savior, man was God's enemy. After becoming a believer, he is God's friend.

John 15:15 say:

> "I no longer call you servants,
> because a servant does not know his master's
> business. Instead, I have called you friends, for
> everything that I learned from my Father
> I have made known to you."

4. Imputation

OUR SIN IS ON THE DEBIT SIDE. ON THE CREDIT SIDE IS GOD'S PAYMENT FOR SIN.

Sanctification is the process of being made holy. Scripture mentions three aspects of our sanctification: the initial sanctification occurring at the time of our salvation, the gradual process of sanctification occurring as we live our lives as believers, and the final or complete sanctification, occurring simultaneously with our resurrection.

The righteousness we are granted at the time of our salvation is positional. It is an imputed righteousness. According to Bauer, Arndt, and Gingrich, the Greek verb for impute, *logizomai*, means to reckon or calculate. It can be an accounting word carrying the idea of "place to one's account" or to credit. Regarding imputed righteousness, *The Holman Illustrated Bible Dictionary* reads as follows:

> "The imputation of righteousness lies at the heart of the biblical doctrine of salvation.
> This righteousness is seen in Christ who purchased redemption. God grants righteousness to those who have faith in Christ …
> This righteousness imputed or reckoned to believers is, strictly speaking, an alien righteousness. It is not the believer's own righteousness but God's righteousness imputed [credited] to the believer[to his account]."

On March 12, 1974, major newspapers ran the story of a Japanese army officer who had hidden in the jungles of Luzon in the Philippines ever since the end of World War II. Because he was not certain that the war was over and had never received orders to surrender, he had lived off the land, with the occasional theft of a local cow. He had wasted thirty years of his life fighting a war which was already over. What a bizarre tragedy!

The Bible pictures unbelievers in much the same situation. Even though Christ ended that war 2000 years ago, at Calvary, they are still holding out against God. Ambassadors for Christ must stand up and announce the good news that the war is over, peace has been achieved and through faith in Christ believers can live in a harmonious relationship with God.

5. Redemption

According to *The Holman Illustrated Bible Dictionary*, the word redeem means:

> "to pay a price in order to secure the release of something or someone. It connotes the idea of paying what is required in order to liberate from oppression, enslavement, or another type of binding obligation. The redemptive procedure may be legal, commercial, or religious."

The main Greek word for *redemption* in the New Testament is **apolutroosis**. Bauer, Arndt, and Gingrich write that the word originally had to do with buying back a slave or captive or making him free by payment of a ransom. A later meaning had to do with release from sin and finiteness that comes through Christ.

> *"In him we have redemption through his blood, the forgiveness of sins, in accordance with the riches of God's grace that he lavished on us with all wisdom and understanding."*
> Ephesians 1:7

> *"For he [the Father] has rescued us from the dominion of darkness and brought us into the*

> kingdom of the Son he loves, in whom we have redemption, the forgiveness of sins."
>
> Ephesians 1:7, 8

Faith Definition
FAITH IS CHOOSING TO LIVE AS THOUGH THE BIBLE IS TRUE REGARDLESS OF CIRCUMSTANCES, REGARDLESS OF EMOTIONS OR REGARDLESS OF CULTURAL TRENDS.

1 Peter 3:18 says:

> *"For Christ also suffered once for sins, the righteous for the unrighteous, to bring you to God. He was put to death in the body but made alive in the Spirit."*

Choosing to live as though the Bible (*"For Christ also suffered once for sins, the righteous for the unrighteous, to bring you to God. He was put to death in the body but made alive in the Spirit,"* 1 Peter 3:18) is the true word of God, the believer can know that Christ suffered for man's sins, the righteous Christ, for the unrighteous man. The Bible says that Christ is alive! One day every believer will live with Him in heaven, but for now, they can walk with Him in spirit. The Doctrine of Reconciliation means that Christ not only took our place on the cross, but He was punished for man's sins so that the believer could be His friend forever.

BARRIER OF SIN

GOD, THROUGH THE SACRIFICE OF HIS SON JESUS, HAS REMOVED THE BARRIER OF SIN, THE BARRIER THAT SEPARATED US FROM

A RELATIONSHIP WITH GOD. NOW THAT THE BARRIER HAS BEEN REMOVED, THE RELATIONSHIP IS SECURE.

God's commitment to us has never changed. Yet, man's side of the relationship had to be reconciled. In John 15:15 Jesus called the believer his friend. Did the believer do anything to deserve being called friend? The answer is no. For the believer, sin can separate him from fellowship with the Father, but for the true believer, the relationship is still secure. God looks at every believer through the lens of Christ' payment on the cross and sees him as a friend.

God reconciled man to Himself. When Jesus died on the cross for all sins, He became the permanent sacrifice. In the Old Testament, God saw the blood of the animal sacrifice as a covering for sin. He now sees the blood of His Son covering the believer's transgressions. Instead of seeing sin, God sees Jesus.

Sin separates man from God. Jesus went to the cross and paid for our sin. The result is that God has now put the believer in a right relationship with Himself. He has, in fact, made the believer right even to the point that God calls him friend.

RECONCILIATION AND RELATIONSHIPS

IF CHRIST HAS MADE THE COMMITMENT OF RECONCILIATION TO ALL CHRISTIANS, HOW SHOULD THE CHRISTIAN RESPOND TO OTHER CHRISTIANS?

Anger toward someone else within the body does not please the Reconciler. Because the believer's sin does not change the Reconciler's attitude or response, a person's sin should not change the believer's attitude or response.

Our responsibility, for what we do, is to do what God says. We are not to treat others based on how they treat us. In Luke 6:28 we are told to bless those who curse us and pray for those who mistreat us.

> "When we are cursed, we bless;
> when we are persecuted, we endure it;
> when we are slandered, we answer kindly."
> 1 Corinthians 4:12b, 13a

PARABLE OF THE PRODIGAL SON

In Luke 15:11-32, the Bible tells a story of the prodigal son. A better name might be the Parable of the Loving Father. The son decided to ask for his inheritance early and leave his family. In his time away from the family, he wasted his money on foolish things; he had no place to live or anything to eat. He went to work slopping the hogs and even thought about eating what they were eating.

The son started thinking about his home and decided to go back there. While the son was a long way off the father saw his son. He was filled with compassion and ran to his son. The father, who had been watching for his son to return, was more concerned with his son's well-being that he was with his own hurt feelings. He welcomed his son, forgave him and celebrated his return. This is a true picture of the Doctrine of Reconciliation. Christians are called to live in harmony in order to reflect the image of God.

In John 17:21 Jesus prays this:
> "I pray that all of these people continue
> to have unity in the way that you, Father,

are in me and I am in you. I pray that they may be united with us so that the world will believe that you have sent me."

Since God has made the Christian, a sinner, His friend, the Christian can be a friend to those who have hurt him with their sin.

> *My student's grandfather listened very carefully to how God could give him hope. When we talked to him about how God wanted to be his friend, we saw a tear roll down his cheek. My student's grandfather hadn't heard the word friend in many years. Through a lengthy conversation and explanation, he chose to pray a prayer asking God to forgive him. That day when my student's grandfather laid his life at the feet of Jesus, he accepted God's friendship. His countenance changed from that grumpy old man, to one of joy. He spent the rest of his days telling everyone that God wanted to be their friend, too.*

GETTING STARTED

The doctrine of reconciliation says that the death of Christ removes the separation between God and man that was caused by man's sin. When Adam sinned, in effect, he declared his independence from his Creator. Reacting to the lies of Satan, he and Eve decided that God was indeed trying to oppress them and prevent them from a full and satisfying life. Furthermore, they believed that God was only bluffing when He said that severe consequences would result from disobedience. So Adam and Eve decided to go it alone. They would seek happiness and fulfillment apart from God.

Not only were Adam and Eve alienated from God by their own selfish choice, but Scripture teaches that Adam's sin was imputed (charged) to the entire human race to come.[17] This is called the doctrine of original sin. We are born in sin. We do not become sinners when we sin; we sin because we are inherently sinners.

Scripture teaches that the death of Christ not only redeems us from the slave market of sin, declares us innocent and satisfies God's righteous attributes through Christ's penal, substitutionary atonement, but His death also brings us into fellowship with God. Note the following Scriptures:

- *... For if, when we were God's enemies, we were reconciled to him through the death of his Son, how much more, having been reconciled, shall we be saved through his life!* (A reference to the mediatorial work of the Great High Priest) (Romans 5:10).

- *All this is from God, who reconciled us to himself through Christ and gave us the ministry of reconciliation: that God was reconciling the world to himself in Christ, not counting men's sins against them. And he has committed to us the message of reconciliation. We are therefore Christ's ambassadors, as though God were making his appeal through us. We implore you on Christ's behalf: Be reconciled to God.* (2 Corinthians 5:18-20).

- *... And through him to reconcile to himself all things, whether things on earth or things in heaven, by making peace through his blood, shed on the cross. Once you were alienated from God and* *were enemies in your minds because of your evil behavior.* (Colossians 1:20-21, cf. Ephesians 2:16).

Memory Verse: Write and memorize 1 Peter 3:18.

_____

_____

_____

> **Core Concept:** The Doctrine of Reconciliation means that Christ not only took our place on the cross, but He was punished for our sins so that we could be His friend fore

CONSIDER

Joel was on trial for a crime he committed. The evidence was overwhelming, and he was quickly declared: "guilty." When the time for sentencing arrived, Joel decided to beg the judge for mercy and give him the lightest sentence possible.

Just as Joel was given the opportunity to speak, his older brother came into the courtroom and walked up to the judge. Even though there was a flurry of activity and frantic whispers at the judge's bench, Joel could not hear anything. Then, the bailiff handcuffed Joel's brother and led him out of the courtroom. The judged then lowered his gavel as he said, "Innocent."

Joel's attorney explained to him that his brother asked the judge to allow him to serve Joel's sentence. Now Joel wasn't just "not guilty," he was innocent. It was as if he had never committed the crime.

Does it seem fair that Joel's brother should have to be punished for Joel's crime?

Why would Joel's brother offer such a sacrifice?

Read the following passages.

2 Corinthians 5:21:

God made him who had no sin to be sin for us, so that in him we might become the righteousness of God.

If you were living as though 2 Corinthians 5:21 were true, how would you be living?

Now fill in the chart below. Note your perception of your experience in the left box, and the truth of God's Word in the right box:

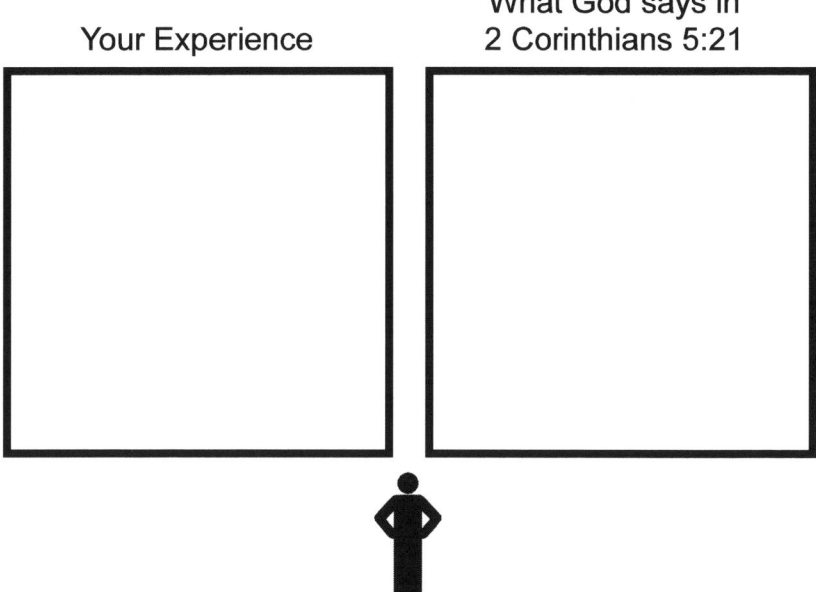

1 Peter 2:23-24:

When they hurled their insults at Him, He did not retaliate; when He suffered, He made no threats. Instead, He entrusted Himself to Him who judges justly. He Himself bore our sins in His body on the tree, so that we might die to sins and live for righteousness; by His stripes you have been healed.

How does the truth of 1 Peter 2:23-24 affect the way you live?

Ron Proctor

Isaiah 53:10a:

Yet it was the LORD's will to crush Him and cause Him to suffer.

How does the truth of Isaiah 53:l0a affect the way you live?

Write a thank you note to God for the work of reconciliation that He was done in your life.

EXPLORE

God, through the sacrifice of Jesus, has removed the barrier of our sin. Now that the barrier has been removed, God has reestablished the relationship. God does not have to be restored to us; His commitment to us has never changed. However, our side of the relationship had to be reconciled.

Read John 15:15. What did Jesus call you?

What did your performance have to do with Jesus calling you "friend?"

If you were living as though John 15:15 was true, how would you be living?

2 Corinthians 5:16-18 states:

So from now on we regard no one from a worldly point of view. Though we once regarded Christ in this way, we do so no longer. Therefore, if anyone is in Christ, he is a new creation; the old one has gone, the new has come! All this is from God, who reconciled us to himself through Christ who gives us the ministry of reconciliation.

God reconciled us to Himself. When Jesus died on the cross for our sins, He became the permanent sacrifice. Just as God saw the blood of the animal sacrifice, He now sees the blood of His Son that is covering our transgressions. He doesn't see our sin; he sees Jesus.[18]

Sin separates us from God. Jesus went to the cross and took our place. Because of His blood that covers our sin, God is now able to look at us through a new lens. The end result is that He has now made us in a right relationship with Him. He has, in fact, made us right even to the point that He has made us His friend. We are now reconciled to God. Therefore, He calls us "friends."

Look at John 15:15 again. Who said, "This is my friend?" First?

How does that make you feel?

If you were living as though you were God's friend, how would you be living?

Look back to 2 Corinthians 5:18-19 and fill in the last blank with your own name. "So from now on we regard no one from a worldly point of view. Though we once regarded Christ in this way, we do so no longer. Therefore, if anyone is in Christ, he is a new creation; the old one has gone, the new has come! All this is from God, who reconciled us to Himself through Christ who gives us the ministry of reconciliation: that God was reconciling the world to Himself in Christ, not counting _____ sins against him (or her)."

If you were living as though 2 Corinthians 5:18-19 were true, how would you be living?

How does it make you feel to know that you have been reconciled to God?

YOUR LIFE TODAY

Now we can apply reconciliation to all our relationships. If Christ has made the commitment of reconciliation to all Christians, how should we respond to other Christians?

Let us look at a specific problem that all of us deal with at one time or another: anger towards someone else within the body of Christ.

DISCUSS: What does your Reconciler think about your anger toward other Christians who have hurt or disappointed you? Does it please Him?

When you sin and make mistakes, does your Reconciler change His attitude or response towards you?

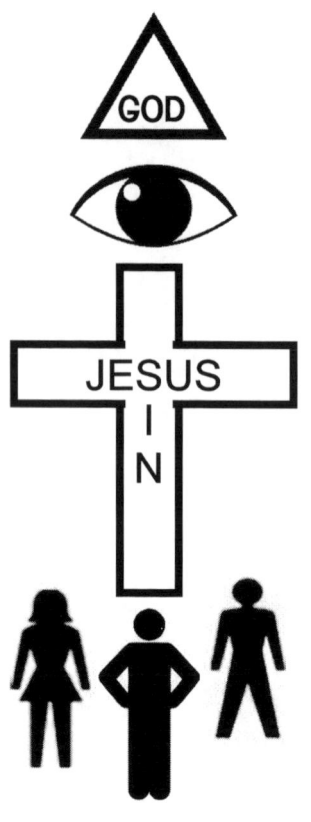

When other Christians hurt you or make you angry, do have a difficult time forgiving them?

Some Christians could answer "yes" to that question, but we must remember that Christ's forgiveness covers all of us.

If you were living as though 2 Corinthians 5:19 is true, how would you be living?

The story in Luke 15:11-32 is a great illustration about the ministry of reconciliation. It is a very familiar parable; it is the story that has been labeled the Parable of the Prodigal Son. If we could rename this story, we would call it the Parable of the Loving Father.

Read Luke 15:11-32.

While the son was a long way off the father saw his son. He was filled with compassion, and ran to his son. The father, who had been watching for his son to return, was more concerned with his son's well being than he was with his own hurt feelings. He welcomed his son, forgave him and celebrated his return. This is a picture of the Doctrine of Reconciliation. Do you have any broken relationships that need to be repaired? Based on what you have learned about reconciliation, make the commitment and take the time to do what you can to repair your broken relationships.

BEFORE YOU FINISH

Consider all the material through which you have just worked, and read the following statement. When you completely agree with the statement, sign on the line.

> I choose to believe by faith that I am certain that God has reconciled me to Himself because Jesus took my punishment for my sin. Since God has made me, a sinner, His friend, I can be a friend to those who have hurt me with their sin.
>
> Signed: _____

---

[17] Romans 5:12
[18] Recall that "Tetelestai" is what Jesus shouted as he was dying on the cross.

NOTES:

CHAPTER FOUR

Totally Innocent of Every Charge

One day John ran into his friend, Sean, on campus and asked if he'd like to get a cup of coffee. They sat down in the coffee shop, and John lowered his head. "What I'm about to tell you is one of the hardest things I've ever had to say. I'm embarrassed." John confessed that he was having a sexual relationship with a young woman. Immediately Sean saw that John was filled with guilt and shame. John needed to understand that he had been justified through Christ's death on the cross. Sean explained that no matter how John saw himself, God saw him just as though he had never sinned. John wept as he tried to grapple with this concept. How could the Almighty God love him so much, even with the sin he had committed?

JUSTIFICATION IS GOD'S LEGAL DECLARATION OF A BELIEVER'S RIGHTEOUSNESS; THE BELIEVER IS COMPLETELY FORGIVEN AND NO LONGER LIABLE TO PUNISHMENT. GOD LOOKS AT THE BELIEVER AS THOUGH HE HAS NEVER SINNED.

To ***justify*** is a legal term meaning to declare someone in right standing with a person or persons. When one is justified in court, he is in right standing with the laws of the land and legally with the citizens of the land. In the biblical context, ***justification*** refers to the act of God whereby He declares a sinner to be just or righteous in His sight because of the imputation of Christ's righteousness to that person. Imputation means to attribute or ascribe from another. Imputation is an act of God, giving His righteousness to man through His Son.

Christ ascribes or imputes or reckons to the Christian His own righteousness. *Sinful man* cannot earn God's favor. In his *Introductory Lectures in Systematic Theology,* Henry Clarence Thiessen writes:

> "Conversion is that turning to God. It consists of two elements, repentance, and faith ... But [man] can of himself neither turn to God, nor repent, nor believe; the only thing prevenient [antecedent, anticipatory] grace enables him to do is to call upon God to turn him."

God's favor is given freely to the repentant sinner because of Jesus' *sacrifice* on the cross. A person cannot earn God's favor by *good works*, through the giving of *earthly treasures*, by serving in the church, or by teaching others about Him.

The Bible teaches that Adam's sin has been imputed, or attributed, to the human race. Scripture also teaches that the sins of the human race were imputed to Christ on the cross. Romans 5:12 says:

> *"Therefore, just as sin entered the world through one man, and death through sin, and in this way death came to all people, because all sinned."*

1 Corinthians 15:21-22 promises this:

> *"For since death came through a man, the resurrection of the dead comes also through a man. For as in Adam all die, so in Christ all will be made alive."*

Sometimes people get caught up in the issue of fairness. Some people believe their sin is greater than the sin of others and cannot be forgiven. Others think their sin is less than the sin of others and don't see how God could forgive those *other* people. The issue of fairness is dissolved in the doctrine of grace. Jesus died to cover all sin, not just some.

The Bible teaches another step of imputation. The moment a Christian puts his trust in Christ, God imputes the righteousness of Christ in him. 2 Corinthians 5:21 says:

"God made Him who had no sin to be sin for us, so that in Him we might become the righteousness of God."

Since God imputed all sin to Christ, He considers the believer to be righteous because of Christ. God now looks at him as being as righteous as Christ, not because the believer behaves well, but because God has credited him with Christ's righteousness.

Philippians 3:8-9 says:

"What is more, I consider everything a loss because of the surpassing worth of knowing Christ Jesus my Lord, for whose sake I have lost all things. I consider them garbage that I may gain Christ and be found in him, not having a righteousness of my own that comes from the law, but that which is through faith in Christ the righteousness that comes from God on the basis of faith."

Faith Definition
FAITH IS CHOOSING TO LIVE AS THOUGH THE BIBLE IS TRUE REGARDLESS OF CIRCUMSTANCES, REGARDLESS OF EMOTIONS OR REGARDLESS OF CULTURAL TRENDS.

After believing that God's Word is all truth, then the believer must understand that sin has been passed down through Adam.

> *"Therefore, just as sin entered the world through one man, and death through sin, and in this way death came to all people, because all sinned."*
> Romans 5:12

God provided a way for man to be justified or made right with Him.

> *"For since death came through a man, the resurrection of the dead comes also through a man. For as in Adam all die, so in Christ all will be made alive."*
> 1 Corinthians 15:21-22

The believer is righteous because of his faith in Christ. He has no righteousness on his own.

> *"God made him who had no sin to be sin for us, so that in him we might become the righteousness of God."*
> 2 Corinthians 5:21

When circumstances cause the believer to feel discouraged, he can stand strong knowing God calls him righteous.

God declares the Christian to be righteous and altogether acceptable in His sight. This declaration is justification. Before Jesus died on the cross, He was righteous and sinless. At that same time, all of mankind was unrighteous and sinful. BUT after Jesus death on the cross, Jesus took on man's unrighteousness and sinfulness so that those who believe in Him can live righteous and sinless. **Everything** changed at the cross! Christians stand justified in God's presence now. The believer is declared righteous by God in His sight, not because of his actions, but because of Christ's death on the cross.

Identity in Christ

People tend to compare themselves to others. They covet others' possessions. They *envy* the talents *possessed by others.* Such comparisons lead to covetousness, competition, and compromised values.

BELIEVERS NEED TO UNDERSTAND THAT EACH CHRISTIAN HAS HIS/ HER OWN UNIQUE COMBINATION OF SPIRITUAL GIFTS.

Instead of seeking identity in the world, the *individual* Christian must learn to *seek his/her* identity in *what* Christ *has done for him.* Because of Christ, the great news is that God sees believers the same way He sees Jesus. That is the doctrine of justification. When God looks at the Christian, He sees him through the cross of Jesus and what He did on that cross.

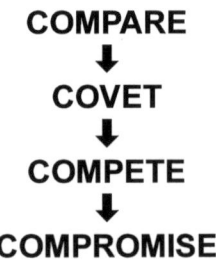

COMPARE
⬇
COVET
⬇
COMPETE
⬇
COMPROMISE

Christians walk in justification and relationship with other Christians. Since God's righteousness has been imputed to the Christian, then every Christian relationship that he has also has that relationship with God. How does that affect his relationships in the church? How does that affect family relationships? Every Christian should look at his brothers and sisters in Christ remembering that although they sin, God has imputed on them His righteousness.

Justification is more than just the subtraction of sins; it is the addition of God's righteousness. Thinking about justification, the believer has to understand that it is more than, "just as if I never sinned." Every bad attitude, every cross word, every immoral thought, every junky thing that the believer has ever done, sent Jesus to the cross. When God looks at the believer, He sees what Christ did on the cross. **The very moment he received Christ, he literally became clothed in the righteousness of Christ.** This means that because of what Christ did on the cross for all, God now has the ability to look at believers through the perfection of Jesus.

Because of Christ's death *on the cross* and the Christian's faith in *His* work, God now looks at *the believer* in the same way that He sees His own Son. That is what the gospel is about, what Christ has done for all. Hebrews 2:11 says:

> *"Both the one who makes people holy and those who are made holy are of the same family. So Jesus is not ashamed to call them brothers and sisters."*

The believer's relationship with God *the Father* is a family relationship; *he has been adopted into God's family!*

Only by faith can one believe the truth of 2 Corinthians 5:21, the Christian becomes righteous through Jesus. It is a life-long process of choosing to believe that one has been forgiven and has received the righteousness of Jesus Christ. Christians may not understand it, and there will be times when they do not feel it, but that does not make the righteousness they have in Christ any less real. In fact, it is in those times of doubt and uncertainty that justification is most needed.

When the believer allows himself to focus on his experience more than the truth of 2 Corinthians 5:21, he will be prone to listen to the lies of Satan, causing him to struggle with guilt and shame. The Devil influences the Christian to *magnify* any negative trait in *his* life. Satan camps out on performance and when the Christian fails to perform up to par, the Devil lets him know it. *Satan is the "accuser of the saints."* Often he works through circumstances, emotions, and cultural trends to let the Christian believe he is not worthy. These negative emotions lead to the Christian beating himself up. That is what Satan wants! Satan wants the Christian to think "I am shameful" and "I am guilty." Satan wants him to stay focused on guilt and shame so that he will not focus on the victorious life that is available to him through Jesus Christ. When the Christian truly accepts that because of the work of the cross he has the righteousness of God, then he will be more focused on God's call to live a life that is pleasing to Him rather than focused on his shame and guilt.

When a Christian chooses to believe God's Word more than his experiences, no matter how tough those experiences may be, God's Word will become true in each experience. This means that instead of believing he is unworthy of God's love because of his sinful life, he will understand that God does not hold his sin against him. The Christian life is not lived out in the emotional arena, or in the circumstantial arena, **BUT IN THE FAITH ARENA.** Choosing to live believing God's Word over experiences will change a person's whole life. It is easy for the Christian to believe that Jesus is holy, sinless, blameless and perfect but very difficult for him to see himself in the same way. He must keep his eyes on what is taught in God's Word.

EVERY MORNING, THE BELIEVER NEEDS TO TURN THE DAY OVER TO THE LORD AND THEN BELIEVE THAT HE TOOK IT. IT GIVES THE CHRISTIAN CONFIDENCE WHEN HE/SHE STEPS OUT IN FAITH. STEPPING OUT IN FAITH PROVIDES THE SECURITY NEEDED TO DEAL WITH THE EVENTS OF THE DAY.

The Doctrine of Justification

The Doctrine of Justification can help the Christian with relationships. If he cannot accept by faith what God has given him, then he will have trouble transferring that to others. Romans 5:1 says:

> *"Therefore, since we have been justified through faith, we have peace with God through our Lord Jesus Christ."*

A person cannot have peace with God and live in an angry, disgruntled relationship. When the Christian truly understands justification, then he can apply that same justification to others, seeing others as if they have never sinned.

Since the Christian has been justified, he has peace with God. Many people live their lives without that understanding. They consequently have not accepted the peace that comes from being justified. If one is not experiencing peace with God, it is not because God has not offered it. Peace is there for the Christian to accept by faith, but it is not something he can earn. In the same way, if the Christian is not experiencing peace, he cannot be experiencing peace with others. **One cannot give away what he does not possess himself.**

What happens when that peace is not present in someone's life? He ends up in a cycle of performance based relationships. When a Christian does not appreciate or accept justification, he could be in danger of wearing a mask that will cause him to act one way in public and another way in private. Wearing a mask will lead to the building up of walls. It could lead to stress in relationships and distrust of others.

1 Peter 3:8-9 says:

"Finally, all of you, be like-minded, be sympathetic, love one another, be compassionate and humble. Do not repay evil with evil or insult with insult. On the contrary, repay evil with blessing, because to this you were called so that you may inherit a blessing."

In today's world is it possible to give a blessing for an insult? It is possible when the believer understands that he has been blessed by Christ. When He died on the cross,

He made Christians right and looks at them differently. Therefore, now Christians can respond to others the way He responds to them. The Christian has been declared innocent and righteous before the living God, and t*here was nothing he could have done to earn it!*

WHAT MOST PEOPLE DO NOT UNDERSTAND IS THAT GOD IS A VERY LOVING AND KIND GOD. HERE'S AN EXAMPLE TO PICTURE THIS MISUNDERSTOOD LOVE.

A friend gives a man and his wife some expensive, huge steaks. The man had to do a job that kept him up all night. He drove home the next morning, exhausted and ready for bed. At the same time, his wife busily prepared a nice, juicy steak and baked potato to surprise him with an anniversary supper when he arrived home. Also as the man was driving closer to his home, a fire truck was blocking the road. Inquiring what was going on, he found out that someone was shooting off bottle rockets and caught his neighbor's roof on fire. This incident caused the man to be delayed even longer. When he arrived at the house, he spoke to his wife and headed straight to bed. Before he dozed off, his wife walked into the room carrying a tray with his perfectly cooked steak and loaded baked potato. He just covered his head. He was not in the mood.

The story may sound absurd, but many Christians are just like that with their understanding of God's kindness. He presents His very best on a silver platter, and it is overlooked, or worse, it is refused. God has declared the Christian righteous, and he does not even realize what a kind act that is. The old song that says God is so good, He's so good to me, is so true. When the Christian begins to realize God's kindness and goodness, then he will be ready to act toward others in the same way.

When a person is in the middle of a relational conflict, God calls him to repay insult with a blessing. The reason is this: God wants the Christian to deal with Him. In the Book of Job, the Sabeans attacked Job's oxen and donkeys; they put his servants to the sword. The Chaldeans swept down on his camels and carried them off; they put his servants to the sword. (Job 1) Satan afflicted Job with painful sores from the soles of his feet to the top of his head. (Job 2) Job did not confront the perpetrators. Job took up his issues with God.

When the Christian returns the insult with a blessing, he forces the issue between the insulter and God, where it should be. GOD CAN HANDLE THE CONFLICT. The Doctrine of Justification points the believer to the cross, to focus upon Jesus. That is where the focus belongs. When the focus is on the cross, God is free to work. If one continues to keep others as the objects of his problems, then it keeps him from dealing with the vertical relationship with God, where it belongs.

THE KEY TO THE DOCTRINE OF JUSTIFICATION: ONE CANNOT FORGIVE OTHERS OR RESPOND TO THEM PROPERLY UNTIL HE EXPERIENCES AND WALKS IN THE UNDERSTANDING AND GRATITUDE THAT GOD HAS FORGIVEN HIM.

Christians are justified. Why does God look at them as though they have never sinned? Because of what Jesus did on the cross. When the believer can keep this in focus, as a hunter keeps the deer in the crosshairs of the scope, it is much easier to deal with the issues of life that come his way.

> Sean became John's accountability partner. They talked every week. John began to put his focus and attention on what Jesus did on the cross instead of on his own failure. He learned to truly accept that he has the righteousness of God through the work of the cross, not anything he did or could do. He began to forgive himself and work toward much-needed healing.

GETTING STARTED

To justify, a legal term, is to declare someone in right standing with a person or persons. When one is justified in court, he is in right standing with the laws of the land and legally with the citizens of the land. In the Biblical context, justification refers to the act of God whereby He declares one to be just or righteous in His sight because of the imputation (to attribute or ascribe from another) of Christ's righteousness to that person. It is of utmost importance to understand that justification is God's declaration of our righteousness!

Let this truth sink in ...

Justification is God's declaration of our righteousness. Praise the Lord for that!

The Scripture teaches that Adam's sin has been imputed to the human race.[14] The Scripture also teaches that the sins of the human race were imputed to Christ on the cross.[15] The issue of "fairness" now dissolves in the doctrine of grace.

Scripture also teaches a third step of imputation. The moment we trust Christ, God imputes the righteousness of Christ to us. 2 Corinthians 5:21 states that after God has imputed our sins to Christ, He considers us to be righteous because of Christ. God now looks at us as being as righteous as Christ, not because we behave well, but because He has credited us with Christ's righteousness. What an amazing concept![16]

He declares us to be righteous and altogether acceptable in His sight. This declaration is justification. Consider the following chart regarding our state of sinfulness and righteousness. Notice the difference between the left and right sides:

BEFORE THE CROSS † THE RESULT OF JESUS' DEATH ON THE CROSS

Jesus	We	Jesus Took On	We Took On
Was Righteous	Were Unrighteousness	Our Unrighteousness	His Righteousness
Was Sinless	Were Sinful	Our Sinfulness	His Sinlessness

Everything changes at the cross!

It is essential to understand that we stand justified in God's presence now. Not because of our actions, but because of Christ's death on the cross, we are declared to be righteous by God in His sight.

Meditate on this statement.

Because of Christ's death on the cross, I am declared righteous by God in His sight.

Ron Proctor

Memory Verse: Write and memorize 2 Corinthians 5:21.

_____

_____

_____

_____

Core Concept: The Doctrine of Justification says that God looks at you a though you never sinned.

CONSIDER

When Leslie and Trey married they were sure they wouldn't be one of those couples who fights, but they were not even married for two years before the arguing started. Leslie stared to work long hours at her law firm and Trey resented that she spent more time with the very people she complained so much about when she was home. Feeling lonely and rejected, Trey started going out with the guys from work. This made Leslie angry that her husband didn't understand the pressure she was under at work and jealous that he was out having fun while she was swimming in paperwork. They both started to wonder if the other was having an affair.

It did not take long for the couple to spend most of what little time they had together arguing and hurling accusations at one another. Even when they were not fighting, they were stewing over the latest argument. They started to wonder what they saw in each other and why they even bothered getting married. They just weren't the people they thought they were. Divorce, they were sure, was imminent. How could they ever recover from all the terrible things they said to one another? With these thoughts and beliefs dominant in their relationship they felt hopeless that reconciliation was possible and divorced. Instead feeling like the problem was resolved, they felt shame and regret.

DISCUSS   What advice would you give Leslie and Trey?

Have you ever experienced a time when the pressures of life made you turn on someone you love?

Have you ever felt so much shame over something you have done or said that you were sure you would never recover?

Like Leslie and Trey, we spend much of our life mired in guilt, shame and condemnation because we do not have a good understanding of who we are. In Conformed to His Image, Ken Boa says that if a person does not have a good identity, he will compare himself to others. Once a person begins to compare himself, he will start to covet what others have. Then that person will start to compete, and competition will lead to compromise.

Compare ⟶ Covet ⟶ Compete ⟶ Compromise

The great news is that, because of Jesus, God sees us the same way He sees Jesus. This is the doctrine of justification.

EXPLORE

> Justification is more than just the subtraction of our sins; it is the addition of God's righteousness.

When you begin to think about Justification, you have to understand that it is more than, "Just as if I have never sinned."

When God looks at us, He sees what Christ did on the cross for us. Think about this particular truth: the very moment that you received Christ, you literally became clothed in the righteousness of Christ. This means that because of what Christ did on the cross for you, God now has the ability to look at you through the perfection of

Jesus. Every bad attitude, every cross word, every immoral thought every junky thing that you have ever participated in, sent Jesus to the cross.

Because of Christ's death, and your faith in this work, God now looks at you in the same way that He sees His own Son. That is what the gospel is about - what Christ has done for us. It is what makes us able to believe the truth of Hebrews 2: 11 that tells us: "Both the one who makes people holy and those who are made holy are of the same family. So Jesus is not ashamed to call them brothers and sisters."

If you understood that God sees you in the same way He sees Jesus, how would you feel about your relationship with Him?

How would you be living?

There is no way that you can believe the truth in 2 Corinthians 5 :21 about yourself except by faith. It is a life-long process of choosing to believe that you have been forgiven, and you have received the righteousness of Jesus Christ. You may not understand it, and there will be times when you do not feel it, but that does not make the righteousness you have in Christ any less real. In fact, it is in those times of doubt and uncertainty that your justification is most needed.

Consider 2 Corinthians 5:21, and fill in the chart below. Note your perception of your experience in the left box, and the truth of God's Word in the right box:

When you allow yourself to focus on your experience more than the truth of 2 Corinthians 5:21, you will be prone to listen to the lies of Satan which will cause you to struggle with guilt and shame. These negative emotions can lead you to "beat yourself up." This is exactly what Satan wants. Satan wants the dialogue in your head to say: "I am shameful," and "I am guilty." Satan WANTS you to stay focused on your guilt and shame so that you will not focus on the victorious life that is available to you through Jesus Christ. When you truly accept that because of the work of the cross you have the "righteousness of God,"

then you will be more focused on God's call to live a life that is pleasing to Him rather than your shame and guilt.

If you were living as though 2 Corinthians 5:21 were true, how would you be living?

When you choose to believe God's Word more than your experience, no matter how tough your experience may be, God's truth will become true in your experience. This means that instead of believing you are unworthy of God's love because of your sinful life, you will understand that God does not hold your sin against you.
The Christian life is not lived out in the emotional arena, or in the circumstantial arena, BUT IN THE FAITH ARENA. If you chose to believe God's Word over your experience, how would that affect your life?

Repeat the following aloud:

I believe that Jesus Christ is:

> *Holy*
> *Sinless*
> *Blameless*
> *Perfect*

Take a few moments to think about this. If the above is true about Christ, how does God see you?

He sees you the same as He sees Jesus.

Meditate on this fact for a few moments.

YOUR LIFE TODAY

DISCUSS: What does the Doctrine of Justification have to do with the way you treat others?

The Doctrine of Justification can help us with relationships. If you cannot accept by faith what God has given to you, then you will have trouble transferring that to others. Think about the previous statement before going further.

Romans 5:1 says, "Therefore, since we been justified through faith, we have peace with God through our Lord Jesus Christ."

If you lived as though Romans 5:1 was true, how would you be living?

Since we have been justified, we have peace with God. Many people live their lives without that understanding. They consequently have not accepted the peace that comes from being justified. If you are not experiencing peace with God, it is not because He has not offered it to you. It is there for you to accept by faith, but it is not something you can earn.

If you are not experiencing peace with God, you cannot be experiencing peace with others because you cannot give to others what you do not posses yourself. Instead, you will end up in a cycle of performance-based relationships. When we do not appreciate and accept Justification, we could be in danger of wearing a mask that will cause us to act one way in public and another way in private. Wearing a mask will lead to the building up of alls between you and others; it could lead to stress in your relationships and distrust of others.

What emotions show up in your life when you do not believe that you ha e the peace that God gives to you?

Read 1 Peter 3:8-9.

If you were living as though 1 Peter 3:8-9 were true, how would you be living?

Is it possible in today's world to give a blessing for an insult? It is when we understand that we have been blessed by Christ. When He died on the cross for us; He made us right and looks at us differently. Therefore, now we can respond to others the way He responds to us.

You have been declared innocent and righteous before the living God, and **you did not have one thing to do with that.**

DISCUSS

Think of a relational conflict that has troubled you recently. How would giving a blessing for an insult help a fragmented relationship?

List some of the ways that returning blessings for insults could impact your relationships.

God wants us to deal with Him. When we return the insult with a blessing, we force the issue between the insulter and God, where it should be. HE CAN HANDLE THE CONFLICT. The Doctrine of Justification points you to the cross to focus upon Jesus. That is where the focus belongs, and when the focus is on the cross, God is free to work. If you continue to keep others as the objects of your problems, then it keeps you from dealing with the vertical relationship between you and God, where it belongs.

You cannot forgive others or respond to them properly until you experience and walk in what it means that God has forgiven you, and you are grateful for that forgiveness. THIS IS THE KEY.

You are justified. Why does God look at you as though you had never sinned? Because of what Jesus did for you on the cross. When you keep this in focus, as a hunter keeps the deer in the crosshairs of the scope, it is much easier to deal with the issues of life that come your way.

BEFORE YOU FINISH

Consider all the material through which you have just worked, and read the following statement. When you completely agree with the statement, sign on the line.

> I choose to believe by faith that I am certain that I am justified and declared righteous because of the sacrifice of Jesus Christ on the cross.
>
> Signed _____

---

[14] Romans 5: 12, 1 Corinthians 15 :21-22
[15] Isaiah 53:4-6,10,12; 1 Peter 2:24; 2 Corinthians 5:21a
[16] Romans 5:17-19; 10:1-4· Philippians 3:9

NOTES:

CHAPTER FIVE

God Now Looks at Me Differently

A young couple, Karen and Daryl, found themselves in turmoil after being married for only a year. When they realized that something about their relationship wasn't working out right, they made a wise decision to seek counsel from an old friend. After much discussion, Charles realized that they were living in a marriage based on expectations of a fifty-fifty performance ratio. She was expected to contribute fifty percent to the relationship, and he was expected to contribute fifty percent. Each of them was expected to give an equal share. Charles talked with them about the emotional baggage such an arrangement produced and explained how they needed to adjust their expectations and focus on what they could do for each other, rather than what they were entitled to receive. Once that decision was made, they could begin to fill each other's emotional cup with love. Charles helped them understand that they were set apart for God. It was time for them to focus more on treating each other unselfishly, based on God's Word, rather than having selfish expectations about what they could get from the relationship. It was time to stop keeping score.

Sanctification

SANCTIFICATION MEANS TO BE SET APART TO GOD. GOD INDWELLS THE CHRISTIAN AND IS IN THE PROCESS OF MAKING HIM HOLY THROUGH THE SACRIFICE OF JESUS CHRIST, ONCE AND FOR ALL.

The term **sanctification** comes from the Greek word *hagios*, which means *"that which is set apart."* In the Old Testament, the sacred vessels used in the temple were *"sanctified,"* or set apart for use only in the temple services. In this life, sanctification means that *believers are set apart to God*. There are three kinds of sanctification: **Positional, Experiential,** and **Ultimate.**

Positional Sanctification refers to the fact that when a person trusts Christ, he becomes set apart unto God. He is no longer a part of the unsaved mass of humanity but now belongs to God as His purchased possession. Ephesians 1:13-14 says:

> *"And you also were included in Christ when you heard the message of truth, the gospel of your salvation. When you believed, you were marked in him with a seal, the promised Holy Spirit, who is a deposit guaranteeing our inheritance until the redemption of those who are God's possession— to the praise of his glory."*

Christians are God's possession marked by the Holy Spirit.

Hebrews 10:10 says:

> *"And by that will, we have been made holy through the sacrifice of the body of Jesus Christ once for all."*

All believers are called *saints*, a very common designation for Christians in the New Testament. The term *holy*, in the positional sense, also applies to all Christians. Not yet holy in *their practice*, but holy in their position; they possess the righteousness of Christ by imputation.

Positional Sanctification is granted to Christians when they *first* accept Jesus Christ as Lord and Savior. They belong to God. They are His purchased possession. Hebrews 10:10-14 is a good text for teaching the Doctrine of Sanctification. It says:

> *"And by that will we have been made holy through the sacrifice of the body of Jesus Christ once for all. Day after day, every priest stands and performs his religious duties. Again and again, he offers the same sacrifices, which can never take away sins. But when this priest had offered for all time one sacrifice for sins, he sat down at the right hand of God. Since that time he waits for his enemies to make his footstool because by one sacrifice he has made perfect forever those who are being made holy."*

God sees the believer as sanctified, set apart, holy. Sin separated man from God. However, Christ's death made it possible for God to look at the believer through the lens of holiness. Once for all, the death of Jesus Christ made this possible. The Christian's position with God is that he is seen as holy. He will be seen as holy for all eternity. When God looks at a Christian, He sees the cross of Jesus Christ and *Christ's righteousness*. God, being infinite, sees infinitely. **When He saw Jesus as He was dying on the cross, He saw every person who would come to Christ from the beginning of time through all eternity.** That is why the Christian can say with Paul, *"I am crucified with Christ."* Each Christian is crucified with Him positionally. When Christians come to know Christ as Lord and Savior, God begins to look at them in this context of holiness.

How does this work? To understand how positional sanctification works, one needs to remember the accounting term *imputation*. When looking at the accounting ledger, one will see that one side has a list of debits and the other side has a list of credits. On a spiritual level, the concept of imputation is the process of God removing items from our debit column and adding items to our credit column. When a Christian received the gift of salvation through Jesus' death on the cross, God chose to impute His own righteousness to the Christian. The Doctrine of Sanctification says that the Christian is in the process of becoming what he already is in God's eyes. Experiential Sanctification is the Christian's spiritual growth as his practice gradually becomes more and more like his position.

Experiential Sanctification is something quite different and must be distinguished from positional sanctification. In other words, Christians are in the process of becoming what they already are. *Over a period of time, their practice more and more closely matches their position.* Experiential sanctification is that process whereby the indwelling Holy Spirit gradually transforms Christians into the image of Jesus Christ. Romans 8:28-30 says:

> *"And we know that in all things God works for the good of those who love him, who have been called according to his purpose. For those God foreknew he also predestined to be conformed to*

the image of his Son, that he might be the firstborn among many brothers and sisters. And those he predestined, he called; those he called, he also justified; those he justified, he also glorified."

The chain of divine working described in those verses makes it certain that every Christian is undergoing experiential sanctification, and that the ultimate goal will eventually be realized at the resurrection.

1 Thessalonians 2:10 says:

"You are witnesses, and so is God, of how holy, righteous and blameless we were among you who believed."

Experiential righteousness is acting holy. In this verse, the Christians were seen as holy, righteous and blameless. If Christians are not acting holy, how can they be seen as blameless? Many times Christians hide in the church behind facades of holiness and live in the world wearing a different mask. Christians are to live out the holiness of God wherever they are living. *Obedience leads to righteousness* (Romans 6:16), *and righteousness leads to holiness* (Romans 6:19).

Some people believe that sanctification is optional for the Christian and that one becomes a Christian by faith but may or may not choose to become a disciple. In the same way, they believe that discipleship is recommended, it is not essential and may be *refused* if one so chooses. This strange *idea* is not based on *Scripture*. Some people will accelerate their rate of sanctification by faithful commitment to Christ and the Word of God (see John 15:1-17). Some, unfortunately, will *constrain* the rate of sanctification by carnality.

Ultimate Sanctification is the completion of sanctification when the Christian is *resurrected*. All who are genuinely saved will eventually be conformed to the image of Christ. In Philippians 1:6, Paul expresses his confidence that *"He who began a good work in you will carry it on to completion until the day of Jesus Christ." When the believer enters into eternity, the process will be complete.* The fact that Christ has declared the Christian to be holy positionally means that He sees the Christian as holy while He is in the process of making him holy. That promise is declared in 1 John 3:2:

> *"Dear friends, now we are children of God, and what we will be has not yet been made know. But we know that when Christ appears we shall all be like him, for we shall see him as he is."*

One day all Christians will be with Jesus and will be like Him. What a great privilege! The Devil wants the Christian to look at his own shame and fears. Eternal sanctification gives the Christian hope.

Cooperating With the Holy Spirit

How does the Christian cooperate with the Holy Spirit in the process of sanctification? Romans 12:1-2 gives the essentials. Romans 12:1-2 means nothing to a person who has no faith.

Faith Definition:
FAITH IS CHOOSING TO LIVE AS THOUGH THE BIBLE IS TRUE REGARDLESS OF CIRCUMSTANCES, REGARDLESS OF EMOTIONS OR REGARDLESS OF CULTURAL TRENDS.

Cooperating with the Holy Spirit begins with choosing to live as though the Bible is true no matter what. The Christian must look at those verses and decide to believe them no matter what circumstance, emotions or cultural trend comes about in his life. He must value the Bible, and that means spending time reading and studying it *at least daily*, allowing God to speak to his heart and entrench his mind with His truths. The Bible brings the Christian power and conviction.

"Therefore, I urge you, brothers and sisters, in view of God's mercy, to offer your bodies as a living sacrifice, holy and pleasing to God—this is your true and proper worship. Do not conform to the pattern of this world, but be transformed by the renewing of your mind. Then you will be able to test and approve what God's will is— his good, pleasing and perfect will."
Romans 12:1-2

Accordingly, the essentials to cooperating with the Holy Spirit begins with the Christian presenting himself or making himself available to God for whatever His will may be. In doing so, he will discover that God's will is good, acceptable, and perfect.

Secondly, the Christian must stop being conformed to this world, or as J.B. Phillips states in his translation: *Stop letting this world squeeze you into its own mold.*

Lastly, the Christian must allow a pattern of transformation to take place in his life. This occurs by the renewing of his mind. **If he wants to live differently, he will have to learn to think differently.** How does he do that? 2 Corinthians 3:18 urges Christians to become more and more like Christ by encountering Him in His Word through the work of the Holy Spirit. *The believer must abide in God's word. He must allow God's Word to permeate* *his inner parts.* The Word becomes like a mirror. As the Christian looks into it, he sees his life and, through the Holy Spirit, he sees what God wants him to see. For the Christian, change occurs when the Word of God becomes empowered by the Holy Spirit.

The Bible gives us several ways we replace the bad information in our brains (in our hearts). It's all part of the process of learning to live in the Spirit.

1. Bible Study and Meditation.
2. Obedience.
3. Prayer.
4. Crucifying the sinful nature.
5. Keeping our minds and hearts on the things of the Spirit, rather than the things of the sinful nature.

Living Free of Satan's Accusations

Sanctification is not performance based. Many church members get caught up in trying to be worthy of God's blessings. They begin to perform in a way they think will make God like them better. Every time they give money in the offering, read their Bible or help with the children's choir, they think they are earning God's favor. The problem is that no matter how many good things they do, they still feel unworthy. As long as the Christian lives this way, he will live in condemnation and trapped in a performance based mentality. In this kind of life, there is no abundant living, no freedom. Satan loves for the Christian to live here. This is not sanctification!

Revelation 12:9-10 says:

*"Then I heard a loud voice in heaven say: Now have come the salvation and the power and the kingdom of our God, and the authority of His Christ. **For the accuser of our brothers, who's accusing them before our God day and night,** has been hurled down."*

Satan is the accuser. He places guilt and shame on the believer. His goal is to come between God and the Christian. One way he does that is by keeping the Christian from understanding the way God sees him. *Satan wants Christians to spend time working for acceptance from God.*

In the fourth chapter of Matthew, Jesus gives the Christian the model for how to deal with the accuser. When Jesus was tempted by Satan, His answer to him was always, "It is written…" Then He would quote a text from the Scriptures. This is how Christians can overcome the accusations of Satan. Here are six steps every Christian can use to fight the accusations made by Satan:

1. Name the mistake or sin.
2. Be reminded that Christ died for all sin, even those for which Satan continues to bring up.
3. Remember that God began to see him as holy on the day he accepted Christ as Savior.
4. Claim by faith God's forgiveness and that God sees him as holy as Jesus.
5. Thank Christ that he is holy in His sight.
6. Whenever the Devil makes accusations, commit to remind the Devil of what happened when Jesus died for the believer on the cross.
7. Forgive all those who have hurt you.

Karen and Daryl began to understand the three aspects of sanctification. They became less focused on themselves and more at peace with their Creator. In doing so, they each became more unselfish and grew closer together in their marriage. They learned how to fill each other's emotional cup.

**When we understand our forgiveness,
it is easier to forgive others.**

GETTING STARTED

The term sanctification comes from the Greek word *hagios*, which means "that which is set apart." In the Old Testament, the sacred vessels used in the temple were "sanctified," i.e. they were set apart for use only in the temple services. In the context in which we are currently interested, sanctification means to be set apart to God. With reference to the Christian, there are two basic kinds of sanctification:

(1) **POSITIONAL SANCTIFICATION** and
(2) **EXPERIENTIAL SANCTIFICATION**.

POSITIONAL SANCTIFICATION refers to the fact that when we trust in Christ, we are set apart unto God. We are no longer a part of the unsaved mass of humanity, but now we belong to God as His purchased possession (Ephesians 1:14). Hebrews 10:10 says: "And by that will, we have been made holy through the sacrifice of the body of Jesus Christ once for all." All believers are called "saints," a very common designation for Christians in the New Testament.

The term "holy," in the positional sense, also applies to all Christians. We are not yet holy in an experiential sense, but we possess the righteousness of Christ by imputation and thus are holy in God's sight.

EXPERIENTIAL SANCTIFICATION is something quite different and must be distinguished from positional sanctification. In other words, we are in the process of becoming what we already are. Experiential sanctification is that process whereby the indwelling Holy Spirit gradually transforms Christians into the image of Jesus Christ (cf. Romans 8:29). The chain of divine working described in Romans 8:28-30 makes it certain that every Christian is undergoing experiential sanctification and that the ultimate goal will eventually be realized - in glorification.

Some people believe that sanctification is optional for the Christian and that one becomes a Christian by faith but may or may not choose to become a "Disciple." Although "discipleship" is recommended, it is not essential and may be bypassed if one so chooses. This strange doctrine is refuted by virtually every sanctification passage. Some of us will accelerate our rate of sanctification by our faithful commitment to Christ and the Word of God. Some, unfortunately, will inhibit the rate of sanctification by carnality, but all who are genuinely saved will eventually be conformed to the image of Christ. In Philippians 1:6, Paul expresses his confidence that "He who began a good work in you will carry it on to completion until the day of Jesus Christ." Eternity will complete the process. The fact that Christ has declared us to be holy positionally, means that He sees us as holy while He is in the process of making us holy.

But how does a Christian cooperate with the Holy Spirit in the process of sanctification? Romans 12:1-2 gives the essentials:

- We must present ourselves (make ourselves available) to God for whatever His will may be. We will discover that God's will is good, acceptable, and perfect.

- We must stop being conformed to this world--or as J.B. Phillips states in his translation: Stop letting this world squeeze you into its own mold.

- We must allow a pattern of transformation to take place in our lives. This occurs by the renewing of our minds. If you want to live differently, you will have to learn to think differently.

But how, specifically, do we do that? 2 Corinthians 3:18 urges us to become more and more like Christ by encountering Him in His Word (the "mirror"), through the work of the Holy Spirit. Always remember that change occurs for the Christian when the Word of God becomes empowered by the Holy Spirit of God.

Memory Verse: Write and memorize Colossians 1:22.

_____

_____

_____

CONSIDER

Ben accepted Christ as his Savior when he was a teenager. However, now in his early forties, he still struggles with guilt, shame and condemnation concerning his sinful behavior as a teenager. He believes the accusations from Satan that he will never be worthy of God's blessings so he begins to perform in a way that he thinks will make God like him better. Every time he gives money in the offering, reads his Bible and helps with the children's choir, he thinks he's earning God's favor. The problem, he is discovering, is that no matter how many good things he does, he still does not feel worthy.

DISCUSS

What do you think will happen to Ben if he does not know how to be free from this condemnation and performance-based mentality?

If Ben does not know how to be free, he will be trapped in a performance-based life, and he will miss the abundant life God has planned for him. How does living a performance-based life affect his relationship with others?

If Ben does not understand his own forgiveness, he is more likely to respond to others who have hurt him with shame, bitterness and avoidance.

Read Revelation 12:9-10 below:

Then I heard a loud voice in heaven say: "Now have come the salvation and the power and the kingdom of our God, and the authority of His Christ. For the accuser of our brothers, who accuses them before our God day and night, has been hurled down."

What is Satan called?

How often does Satan accuse the believer?

Where does Satan accuse the believer?

Yes, Satan reminds of our mistakes; he blames us. He places guilt and shame on us, and he accuses us. His goal is to come between God and us, and one very effective way he does that is by keeping us from understanding how God sees us. We can spend our time working for an acceptance with God which we already have, and that would please Satan greatly.

In the fourth chapter of Matthew, Jesus gives us the model for how we are to deal with the accuser. Every time Satan approached Jesus, Jesus' response was,

"It is written ... " Then, Jesus would quote a text from the Scriptures. This is how we, too, can overcome the accusations of Satan.

Take some time and think about those mistakes for which that Satan accuses you, then go through the following process:

1. What are those mistakes?

2. Did Christ die you all your sins (even those for which Satan still accuses you)?

3. How did God begin to see you at the cross when you accepted Him?

4. Claim, by faith, God's forgiveness and that He sees you as holy as Jesus.

5. Thank Christ that you are holy in His sight.

6. Commit to remind the Devil of what happened to you when Jesus died for you on the cross whenever he accuses you.

EXPLORE

Many people define sanctification as, "to sanctify, to set apart." The root word of sanctification, in the original language, is "hagios." "Hagios" means, "That which is set apart for a specific purpose."

The Doctrine of Sanctification is like a two-sided coin. The first side is positional sanctification, and the second side is experiential sanctification.

Positional Sanctification is the position we have when we come to accept Jesus as our Savior. We belong to God. We are His purchased possession. Hebrews 10:10-14 is a good text for teaching the Doctrine of Sanctification. It says: "And by that will, we have been made holy through the sacrifice of the body of Jesus Christ once for all. Day after day, every priest stands and performs his religious duties. Again and again he offers the same sacrifices, which can never take away sins. But when this priest had offered for all time one sacrifice for sins, he sat down at the right hand of God. Since that time he waits for his enemies to be made his footstool, because by one sacrifice he has made perfect forever those who are being made holy. "

God sees us as sanctified, set apart and made holy.

Sin separated us from God; however, Christ's death is what made it possible for God to look at us through the lens of holiness.

The death of Jesus Christ, once for all, made this possible. One of the by-products of the crucifixion of Jesus Christ is positional sanctification, and our position which we hold with God is that we are seen as holy. And we will be seen as holy for all eternity.

Give four adjectives that describes the word "holy."
1.
2.
3.
4.

You probably answered righteous, perfect, blameless and sinless. When God looks at you, He sees the cross of Jesus Christ and you through Christ.

God, being infinite, sees infinitely. So when He saw Jesus as He was dying on the cross, He saw every person who would come to Christ from the beginning of time. We can say with Paul, "I am crucified with Christ," because we were crucified with Him positionally. When you came to know Christ as your Lord and Savior, God began to look at you in this context of holiness.

Debit	Credit

You may be asking yourself: *How does this work?* To understand how positional sanctification works, we need to remember an accounting term called "imputation." When you look at accounting ledger, you will see that one side has a list of debits, and the other side has a list of credits. The whole concept of imputation is that you move

Ron Proctor

Debit	Credit

a debit to the credit column, or vise versa. When you received the gift of salvation through Jesus' death on the cross, God chose to impute His righteousness from Himself to you.

Read Romans 5:12-13 in the NIV translation and fill in the blanks with the correct words.

"Therefore, just as _____ entered the world through one man, and death through sin, and in this way death came to all men, because all _____ - for before the law was given, sin was in the world. But sin is not taken into _____ when there is no law."

Was sin imputed to mankind?

Yes. It was. Through whom was sin imputed to us?

Adam imputed sin to us. Was righteousness imputed to mankind?

Yes. It was. Through whom was righteousness imputed to us?

Christ imputed righteousness to you.

To elaborate on these questions, read 1 Corinthians 15:21-22 in the IV translation and fill in the blanks with the correct words.

For since _____ came through a man, the _____ of the dead also comes through a man. For as in Adam all die, so in Christ all will be made alive.

Sin was imputed into your account from Adam, so when you were born you had a problem of sin. Because of your sin, when God looked at you, His holiness was off ended. You needed the righteousness of Jesus.

Here is the picture:

Debit	Credit
sin	

Sin was imputed into your account through the original state in the Garden of Eden.

When you came to Christ, the righteousness of Jesus Christ was imputed into your account. Your faith in Jesus Christ as your Savior is the key to your righteousness.

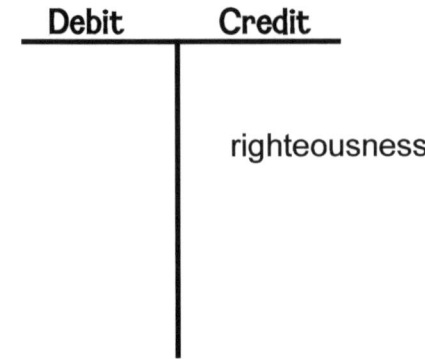

This process can also look like the following:

BEFORE THE CROSS

THE RESULT OF JESUS' DEATH ON THE CROSS

Jesus	We	Jesus Took On	We Took On
Was Righteous	Were Unrighteousness	Our Unrighteousness	His Righteousness
Was Sinless	Were Sinful	Our Sinfulness	His Sinlessness

DISCUSS

Some believe that they will become righteous when they get to Heaven. That is only partly true. When do we have righteousness imputed to us?

You became positionally righteous the moment you received Christ as you savior. What would cause someone to believe that we become righteous only when we get to Heaven?

The Doctrine of Sanctification says that you are what you are in the process of becoming what you already are in God's eyes. God looks at you through a lens of holiness, and He is in the process of making you to become holy. Plus, He has seen you as holy since the moment of your salvation, and He will continue to see you as such throughout eternity.

DISCUSS In light of what God has allowed you to experience through the Doctrine of Sanctification, how should you treat others?

YOUR LIFE TODAY

We have covered the five doctrines of the cross in this study. Go back now and review each lesson. It is natural and common for people to finish a study on the doctrines of the cross with a new outlook on God, life and relationships. We encourage you to apply all the above information to all of your relationships. We would be remiss, however, to give you information without showing you how to practice it. No study about the doctrines of the cross is complete without a glimpse into the role of the Holy Spirit in our lives.

Set aside some time to read over the following verses and meditate on the truth of each verse. Then answer the question that follows.

1 John 2:2:

He is the atoning sacrifice for our sins, and not only for ours but also for the sins of the whole world.

What does it mean to live as though God is satisfied with you because of the death of Jesus?

Ephesians 3:12:

In him and through faith in him we may approach God with freedom and confidence.

When someone understands that they can approach God with confidence, how would that impact his or her relationship with Him?

2 Corinthians 5:20:

We are therefore Christ's ambassadors, as though God were making his appeal through us. We implore you on Christ's behalf: Be reconciled to God.

What does it mean to live a life as God's ambassador?

Hebrews 2:11:

Both the one who makes people holy and those who are made holy are of the same family. So Jesus is not ashamed to call them brothers and sisters.

What does it mean to your life that God has made Jesus to be your brother?

Hebrews 10:10:

And by that will, we have been made holy through the sacrifice f the body of Jesus Christ once for all.

If you were living as though you believed God saw you as holy, how would you be living?

Hebrews 10:14: God is in the process of making me to be how I am already seen by Him.

For by one sacrifice he has made perfect forever those who are being made holy.

What does it mean to fully grasp the truth that God is making you into the person He sees when He looks a t you?

2 Corinthians 5:21:

God made him who had no sin to be sin for us, so that in him we might become the righteousness of God.

If you could really grasp the truth that you are clothed in God's righteousness, how would that change the way you lived?

Ephesians 1:5:

... He predestined us for adoption to sonship through Jesus Christ, in accordance with his pleasure and will.

John 3:16:

For God so loved the world that he gave his one and only Son, that whoever believes in him shall not perish but have eternal life.

Since God loves you unconditionally, how should you respond to Him and others?

Romans 6:4:

We were therefore buried with him through baptism into death in order that, just as Christ was raised from the dead through the glory of the Father, we too may live a new life.

Are you living out the new life God has given you? If not, what would it look like if you did?

1 Corinthians 6:11:

And that is what some of you were. But you were washed, you were sanctified, you were justified in the name of the Lord Jesus Christ and by the Spirit of our God.

God has declared you to be innocent. How should that impact your life?

Galatians 3:13:

Christ redeemed us from the curse of the law by becoming a curse for us ...

What is the best thing about living a life that has been redeemed by Christ?

Romans 5:10:

For if, while we were God's enemies, we were reconciled to him through the death of his Son, how much more, having been reconciled, shall we be saved through his life!

If you lived as though God was your friend, how would you be living?

2 Peter 1:3:

His divine power has given us everything we need for a godly life through our knowledge of him who called us by his own glory and goodness.

What does a life lived in God's divine power look like?

BEFORE YOU FINISH

Consider all the material through which you have just worked, and read the following statement. When you completely agree with the statement, sign on the line.

> I am forgiven. When I struggle with guilt, shame and condemnation, I will by faith choose to believe God looks at me through the lens of the cross and sees the work of Christ for all my sin.
>
> Signed: _____

CONCLUSION

After finishing lesson 5 in *Forgiveness: Fact or Fiction*, I was convinced that God had forgiven me for all my sins. Although at times I struggled with guilt, shame, and condemnation because I chose to trust my circumstances over the truth of Holy Scripture. One of the issues in my life was that my circumstances had sometimes trumped what God was saying in His Word. I love the fact that God had declared me forgiven of every sin. Sometimes I still struggled with what had been put into the bottom of my emotional cup.

For example, for years I had let the content of my emotional cup keep me from believing the truths about my forgiveness according to the Word of God. Often I would let my anger, bitterness, and retaliation spew onto my family or those close to me. The facts were that the contents of my emotional cup took over my life. I would let the emotions respond to my hurt, disappointment, and sadness.

The key to allowing the truth of Holy Scripture influence my behavior over my emotions was to understand the Cross of Jesus Christ. To focus on the Cross meant that I look to the Cross and what Jesus had done for me instead of looking to my circumstances. When I focused on the Cross, I kept in front of me the truth of my forgiveness instead of my hurt and pain.

Faith is the key to helping me in this process. I must make the decision to trust the Word of God, and that trumps all my circumstances and emotions. When I do this, I live in freedom over the bondage of my circumstances and emotions and I can forgive others.

FINAL THOUGHTS

After reading a book like this, your mind begins to race with thoughts. Those thoughts probably come to you in the form of questions.

1. Am I really saved? (Do I know Jesus Christ?)

If you are not certain about Jesus Christ living in your heart, then I recommend that you think about praying the sinner's prayer and receiving Christ into your life.

Jesus,

I want to know you personally. I admit that I have sinned against You and am separated from You. Thank you for dying on the cross for my sins. I open the door of my life and receive You as my Savior and Lord. Thank you for giving me eternal life and making me part of Your family. Take control of my life. Make me the person You created me to be.

2. Am I walking free from condemnation?

If you know Christ and are in need of walking free from accusations and condemnation, then you might pray this prayer.

Dear Jesus,

I need You. I acknowledge that I have been directing my own life and that, as a result, I have sinned against You. I thank You that you have forgiven my sins through Christ's death on the cross. I now invite Your Holy Spirit to take His place again on the throne of my life. Fill me with the Holy Spirit as You have commanded me to be filled and as You promised in Your Word that You would do if I asked in faith. As an expression of my faith, I thank You for directing my life and for filling me with the Holy Spirit.

When we understand our forgiveness, it is easier to forgive others.

About the Author

Ron Proctor was educated at Dallas Baptist University, Southwestern Baptist theological Seminary, and Dallas Theological Seminary. He has been teaching and mentoring at Dallas Baptist University for many years. He is the husband of Della, the father of Deborah, Josh, and Kelly (daughter-in-law), and grandfather of nine.